YO-CCH-157

Δ The Triangle Papers: 50

MANAGING THE INTERNATIONAL SYSTEM OVER THE NEXT TEN YEARS:
THREE ESSAYS

A Report to
The Trilateral Commission

Authors: BILL EMMOTT
Editor, *The Economist*

KOJI WATANABE
Senior Fellow, Japan Center for
International Exchange; Executive
Advisor, Keidanren; former Japanese
Deputy Minister for Foreign Affairs

PAUL WOLFOWITZ
Dean, Nitze School of Advanced
International Studies, Johns Hopkins
University; former U.S. Under Secretary
of Defense for Policy

published by
The Trilateral Commission
New York, Paris and Tokyo
July 1997

The Trilateral Commission was formed in 1973 by private citizens of Western Europe, Japan, and North America to foster closer cooperation among these three democratic industrialized regions on common problems. It seeks to improve public understanding of such problems, to support proposals for handling them jointly, and to nurture habits and practices of working together among these regions.

© Copyright, 1997. The Trilateral Commission
All Rights Reserved.

Library of Congress Cataloging-in-Publication Data

Emmott, Bill
　　　Managing the international system: three essays/Bill Emmott, Koji Watanabe, Paul Wolfowitz.
　　　　　p.cm—(A report to the Trilateral Commission: 50)
　　　　　ISBN 0-930503-76-7

　　　1. International relations. 2. Japan—Foreign relations—1989-
3. Peaceful change (International relations) I. Watanabe, Koji.
II. Wolfowitz, Paul. III. Trilateral Commission.
IV. Title. V. Series: Triangle papers: 50.
JZ1242.E48 1997
327—dc21

　　　　　　　　　　　　　　　　　　　　　　　　　　97-20422
　　　　　　　　　　　　　　　　　　　　　　　　　　CIP

Manufactured in the United States of America

THE TRILATERAL COMMISSION

345 East 46th Street	c/o Japan Center for	35, avenue de Friedland
New York, NY 10017	International Exchange	75008 Paris, France
	4-9-17 Minami-Azabu	
	Minato-ku	
	Tokyo, Japan	

The Authors

BILL EMMOTT is Editor of *The Economist*. After studying politics, philosophy and economics at Magdalen College, Oxford, he moved to Nuffield College to do postgraduate research concerning the French Communist Party's spell in government in 1944-47. Before completing that research, however, he joined *The Economist*'s Brussels office, writing about EEC affairs and the Benelux countries. In 1982 he became the paper's Economics correspondent in London and the following year moved to Tokyo to cover Japan and South Korea. In mid-1986 he returned to London as Financial Editor; in January 1989 he became Business Affairs Editor, responsible for all the paper's coverage of business, finance and science. He was appointed to his present post in March 1993. Mr. Emmott has written three books on Japan: *The Sun Also Sets: the Limits to Japan's Economic Power* (1989); *Japan's Global Reach: the influence, strategies and weaknesses of Japan's multinational corporations;* and *Kanryo no Taizai* (The Bureaucrats' Deadly Sins, 1996).

KOJI WATANABE has had a distinguished career in the Japanese Ministry of Foreign Affairs. He was Japanese Ambassador to Russia from 1994 to 1996 and Ambassador to Italy from 1992 to 1993. Prior to his service in Rome and Moscow, he was Deputy Minister for Foreign Affairs, Sherpa for the G-7 Houston and London summits of 1990 and 1991, and Japanese co-chairman of the US-Japan Structural Impediments Initiative talks. Mr. Watanabe joined the Foreign Ministry upon graduating from the University of Tokyo in 1956. Earlier postings included service as Director-General of the Information Analysis, Research and Planning Bureau and Director-General of the Economic Affairs Bureau. He was a Visiting Fellow at the Woodrow Wilson School of Princeton University (1957-58) and at the Center for International Affairs of Harvard University (1973-74). His other overseas posts include Counsellor at the Japanese Embassy in Saigon (1974-76); Minister at the Japanese Embassy in Beijing (1981-84); and Japanese Ambassador to Saudi Arabia (1988-89). He is now Senior Fellow at the Japan Center for International Exchange and Executive Advisor to the Japan Federation of Economic Organizations (Keidanren).

PAUL WOLFOWITZ became the Dean of Johns Hopkins University's Paul H. Nitze School of Advanced International Studies (SAIS) in 1994, after more than twenty years of US government service. In the Bush Administration, Amb. Wolfowitz was Under Secretary of

Defense for Policy. In the Reagan Administration, he was Ambassador to Indonesia (1986-89), Assistant Secretary of State for East Asian and Pacific Affairs (1982-86), and Director of Policy Planning for the Department of State (1981-82). He was Deputy Assistant Secretary of Defense (Regional Programs) in 1977-80 and held a variety of positions in the US Arms Control and Disarmament Agency during the period 1973-77, including Special Assistant for the Strategic Arms Limitation Talks. In 1993 Dr. Wolfowitz was the George F. Kennan Professor of National Security Strategy at the National War College. In 1980-81 he was Visiting Associate Professor and Director of Security Studies at SAIS. In 1970-73, he held the position of Assistant Professor of Political Science at Yale University. Dr. Wolfowitz was educated at Cornell University and the University of Chicago.

Preface

Unlike most reports to the Trilateral Commission, this volume is composed of three individual, independently prepared essays. The authors were asked to reflect on the challenges, over the next ten years or so, of managing the international system and of democratic industrialized societies in that system. Within very broad guidelines, each author was invited to pick the themes and issues of most importance and interest in his own view.

The authors were not asked to write about the Trilateral Commission. Their views of the management of the international system in the coming years, however, cast light on the Commission's underlying rationale and the needed thrusts of our future work. This project was in part inspired by the need to re-examine the utility and outlines of a "Trilateral" approach to management of the international system, given remarkable ongoing changes in the world as we look toward the next three years of our work.

Table of Contents

Managing the International System Over the Next Ten Years

Bill Emmott

A NEW ORDER FOR THE NEW WORLD?

Almost eight years after the fall of the Berlin Wall in effect signalled the end of the Cold War, the shape of world power and of international relations, broadly defined, is no clearer. This is a source of frustration to many academics, journalists and other commentators, who have tried to discover a new analytical order with which to replace the bipolar simplicity of the four decades of cold war. This desire to find a clear framework, with which to predict the future and through which to organize the world into friends and foes, is powerful and natural. But such a desire is mistaken at best, dangerous at worst. The only defining characteristic of today's world, and of what little we know of tomorrow's, is lack of clarity, amid a diverse range of potential threats and opportunities. The contention of this essay is that efforts to manage the international system should be guided by that very lack of clarity, and not by any presumed analytical pattern, either in the present or in the future.

Since 1989, plenty of new patterns have been suggested. One popular idea, which sprang up shortly after the wall came down, was three-blocism: the idea that the world would now divide into three large regional spheres of influence, each dominated or led by one of the Trilateral partners and defined by trade flows and institutions rather than by those of security, at least initially. The United States would establish a bloc of the Americas; the European Union would extend its reach eastwards towards the Urals, and perhaps even southwards into North Africa; and Japan would, by design or default, lead a regional bloc of the fast-emerging East and Southeast Asian economies. To many people, perhaps carrying in their minds a gentler version of America's Monroe Doctrine of a century-and-a-half ago, this looked so natural and inevitable that the only objection seemed to be one of concern at what would happen to those countries left out of these three, powerful blocs, such as Africa or Central Asia.

Another, more nihilistic idea that sprang up at the same time was Francis Fukuyama's notion that the forthcoming period could be characterized as one following "the end of history": that ideological and even nationalistic rivalry would now cease, to be replaced by purely materialistic economic competition. Expressed more positively by those such as Kenichi Ohmae, this notion also gave rise to predictions that the free flow of capital and technology across borders that was now possible would in the future spell the end of the nation-state, and with it would arise a convergence of aspirations and actual policies towards an open, global capitalism in which economics, and the drive to raise living standards, would transcend politics. Communities of interest would still form themselves and would be important, but these would no longer be defined by the artificial borders of the nation-state but rather by economic groupings.

Recently, however, both of these frameworks have gone out of favor. Three-blocism has faded because the development of all three blocs has proved to be far slower and more troublesome than was expected, and because budding participants, whether major powers or minor ones, have continued to prefer multilateral, global solutions when such solutions have been available. The separatism of the Monroe Doctrine has, thankfully, not proved attractive.

So far, the modest development of both the Asian and the North American trading agreements has been in a form open to global trade rather than on an exclusive regional basis, and the European Union has not fulfilled fears of a "fortress Europe." Most important of all, the United States has shown no sign of withdrawal from Europe's security and defense arrangements, while in Asia it has, if anything, become more deeply engaged in both security and economic matters. The three trading blocs are there (or on their way there), and many (notably in Europe) still advocate their development in the hope that their region will thereby increase its sway in world affairs, particularly in comparison with the United States. Nevertheless, many member countries feel themselves tugged in several directions at once. For that reason, regional blocs do not seem to form a solid basis either for analysis or for power politics itself.

In their turn, the end of history and the associated tendency towards starry-eyed globalism have fallen out of favor both because of an inherent lack of plausibility and because conflict in Bosnia, aggression by Iraq and growing tensions surrounding China (among other events) confirmed that these notions offered no real analytical insight. There has been history aplenty. Most of the events and tendencies that have mattered lay outside these theories' purview. Some trends and relationships proved to be driven by economics and to transcend borders, but many did not. All that "the end of history" told us was that the ideological cold war was over. But we knew that already.

Into this analytical vacuum has now plunged Professor Samuel Huntington of Harvard University, with his 1996 book *The Clash of Civilizations and the Remaking of World Order,* an expansion of a 1993 article in *Foreign Affairs.* Professor Huntington's ideas have provoked much recent controversy, both favorable and critical, centering on his notion that the world today can be divided into five major "civilizations" or cultures, and that future conflicts may well take place between those cultures. Of most immediate apparent relevance to the Trilateral Commission is the fact that Professor Huntington places Japan in a different cultural group than America and Europe, and therefore appears to suggest that the Trilateral alliance will not endure. But of much greater importance for the current purpose is a different point about the Huntington thesis.

This is that the thesis is essentially based on a negative, or contrarian, observation rather than a positive prognostication. Professor Huntington's stalking horse is the popular idea that all cultures are rapidly, ineluctably and even enthusiastically converging on Western values, symbolized by Coca-Cola but given formal expression through democracy, the rule of law and individual human rights. He rejects this idea. He argues instead that such Western values are peculiar to the West, and are not universally applicable. Moreover, he thinks that the growing attempt by the West to spread and impose these values on other cultures will itself provoke conflict.

To the common (and powerful) objection that neither peoples nor countries in fact define themselves or their interests along cultural lines, Professor Huntington responds that to find such definition you need to delve below the surface, and that his thesis is that stronger, more overt cultural definition is likely to be the future consequence of today's Western cultural imperialism. His book can best be understood as a warning of the dangers of such an outcome, and against the continuation of Western cultural imperialism.

So does cultural conflict, between Islam and the West, or Confucianist Asia and other civilizations, offer a helpful framework for understanding the future, and planning for it? It does not, except in a limited sense. The Huntington thesis is merely a warning about one possible future for international relations, picking on one possible source of conflict. Whether it proves right or wrong in the future cannot be known, but is anyway beside the point. For that point is that Professor Huntington's vision is incomplete. There are plenty of other potential sources of conflict besides the one that he has identified. An effort to base the management of international relations on the Huntington thesis would court disaster, for it would fail to take account of the many other sources of conflict that are also likely to exist.

HOW, THEN, CAN TODAY'S WORLD BE DESCRIBED?

There have been other attempts to define the present and the future, and doubtless others will be invented and will attain brief periods of popularity. But such efforts are likely to prove fruitless. For the world has moved and is moving in a direction that defies such efforts at simplification. This makes an author's task more difficult, especially perhaps for this author. After all, Geoffrey Crowther, arguably *The Economist's* greatest twentieth-century editor, declared in the 1950s that the correct technique for an *Economist* writer was "to simplify, then exaggerate." That technique is not, unfortunately, available for this essay. But that is apposite. It is also not available for the management of the international system.

If there is no order, how can the new world be described and understood? Despite the self-denying ordinance just outlined, a little simplification can help, as long as it is not exaggerated. Although no period of history can in truth be characterized as "normal" or "natural," it may nevertheless assist an understanding of current trends in the world if those terms are used, at least as a contrast with the recent past.

The Cold War, with its ideological character, imposed upon the world a political and economic map that was highly artificial. Recent years have seen a number of movements away from that map and towards a more natural one, if by "natural" one can mean a tendency that is, like evolution itself, the consequence of a variety of complex forces rather than of a single, dominant, force.

For example, the Cold War prevented many neighboring countries from trading with one another, or from making cultural and political exchanges, when such things would otherwise have been likely to occur. It suppressed some local conflicts, and stoked up others when conflicts were strategically advantageous to one of the superpowers. It conspired in the preservation of the world's largest country, China, in the state of backwardness and poverty in which it had already languished for a century or more. It also tempted the world's second largest country, India, down the unsatisfying and unproductive roads of Nehruvian socialism, protectionism and non-alignment after it attained its independence from Britain in 1947. In the developed world, too, the Cold War probably contributed to the preservation and indeed encouragement of the collectivist instinct for far longer and to a much greater level than would otherwise have been the case. And, because of the clear and present danger the Soviet threat represented on a global scale, the Cold War created a trilateral alliance between the United States, Western Europe and Japan that would otherwise have had no overwhelming reason to exist.

Combined with the unnatural force of the Cold War was a somewhat unnatural consequence of the century's two world wars: the vast economic and military primacy of the United States in the 1950s. Thanks to war-time destruction elsewhere, America held a certainly unsustainable and probably undesirable lead compared with the other powers. Although this helped to keep America engaged in Europe and the Pacific and is largely responsible for the peaceful conduct of most of the Cold War, it also had some undesirable consequences: it turned American dominance into something widely feared and opposed, particularly in Latin America but also, to a lesser extent, in Europe; and, as America's lead inevitably diminished in the 1970s and 1980s, it led to a spate of pessimism and "declinism" in America, which was in part expressed through a revival of calls for trade protection and a shift towards a more selfish unilateralism in foreign economic and security policy.

In fact, it might fairly be said that, in these sorts of terms, the whole of the twentieth century has been "unnatural." For what also separates this century's final decade from all its nine previous ones are three simple facts: that no substantial country is either at war with another or actively threatening a war; that no country currently believes that it can attain dominance over a substantial slice of the globe; and that the prevailing tendency virtually throughout the world is to lower national barriers to trade and investment rather than to raise or to preserve them.

This exceptional state of affairs shows that perhaps this essay's use of the words "natural" and "normal" are not to be taken too literally. Nevertheless, in the sense of a freeing up of economic forces from political constraints, the terms do hold. Certainly, the habit of trading with and interacting with neighbors has returned, in Eastern Europe, in Asia (with China and formerly socialist and xenophobic India), in Latin America (between formerly authoritarian xenophobes) and in Southern Africa. Several billion people have returned to the international economy after decades shut away from it. Hence the growth of regionalism, not as an effort to hide from the world but rather as a means to exploit potential exchanges and connections that had been thwarted for decades.

Beginning well before 1989, with the death of Mao and the ascent of Deng in the mid-1970s, China has been opening its economy to market forces and to foreign trade and investment. As a result, it has at last made progress towards resuming its natural place as one of the world's largest economies; it was, after all, the world's biggest manufacturer and probably even its biggest economy until overtaken by Britain in the early 19th century. China's consistent double-digit rates of growth in the 1980s and 1990s have made it an increasingly important trading partner not only for the West but also for its neighbors, and have naturally given it both the means and the motive to revive its interest in territorial claims surrounding its borders. That interest, and the tensions associated with it, should not, however, obscure the basic point: that poverty, backwardness and isolation ought to be seen as unnatural states of affairs for China; greater wealth, a greater importance in regional and global trade, and a greater significance in regional and world affairs are all more natural.

Collectivism, whether in the former Communist countries, or in developing countries, or in the industrialized world, has been on the decline both because it has been in intellectual disrepute and because it has ceased to serve a clear political purpose. The past seven years have seen a worldwide trend of privatization of state-owned enterprises, widespread efforts to shrink the role of the state in economic and even social life, and, in the developing world, a greatly increased desire to open borders to freer trade and to flows of foreign capital.

And, naturally enough, the glue that has bound together the Trilateral alliance has begun to weaken. What is remarkable is how little it has weakened rather than how much. Nevertheless, weaken it certainly has, as tensions over trade or other economic issues have no longer been readily contained by the sense of clear and present danger represented by the Soviet Union. The most serious recent instances came in 1995, when the United States and Japan went to the brink of a trade war over cars, and in 1996 with the row between the United States, on one side, and Canada and the European Union, on the other, over America's Helms-Burton legislation concerning Cuba.

SIX THEMES IN THE NATURAL 1990s

To describe these movements during the twentieth century's final decade as being "natural" is not, however, to assign to them a sense of order. Just the reverse. Economic theory, it is true, talks of movements towards states of equilibrium. And economics, it is true, has recently played a growing part in international affairs. But that is chiefly because, for political, policy and security reasons, its role and the free interplay of market forces were suppressed for so long. In any case, the notions of equilibrium and convergence in economics are misleading: they are no more than intellectual constructions, useful for simplification but less useful for policy-making. Real-world economics is concerned primarily with disequilibrium. Such disequilibrium occurs because economics can never be separated from people and politics.

The new order of the world is disorder, or at least absence of order. The disorder of today can usefully be sorted into six main pigeonholes, or themes. These are chosen for their significance for the present and future task of managing the international system, not because they are the only six themes that can be discerned.

1. Diffusion of Military Power

Although the Cold War was never as neatly bipolar as it may seem in retrospect, power today is nevertheless defined by its dispersal more than by its concentration.

The United States stands out as the world's only combat-ready military superpower, and maintains its position as the world's largest economy and as the clear technological leader. That technological lead looks about to lengthen, substantially, thanks to advances in satellite and other sensing technology. But although America's military advantage, both in terms of quantity and quality of deployable force, has lengthened compared with any single rival, several things make that lead less significant than it might seem.

The basic reason is that the deterrent effect of nuclear weapons has diminished because potential threats are now more local than global. Mutually assured destruction has a powerful effect when pitting one superpower against another, but is less relevant when rivals are less equal and have aims that are regional or local rather than global. Also, the political willingness in America to deploy force abroad has become erratic, sometimes encouraging actual or potential troublemakers by its absence, sometimes offering them decisive discouragement by its presence. And, with no single enemy, the objectives associated with the deployment of force have become less easy to define in all but the short term.

The war in the former Yugoslavia offered an unmagnificent case study in the limits of superpower dominance. Throughout the war, America's views and possible actions played an important role. But military intervention was politically controversial at home, would have been logistically hazardous and would always have been hampered by the lack of a clear long-term objective. In the end, American leadership in the Dayton accords did bring the war to a close; but even that took place probably because the warring parties were exhausted and because, for Serbia and Croatia at least, little further could be gained by fighting on.

America's military lead, in other words, cannot readily be translated into global dominance, nor readily be used to secure global peace. It remains important, and can be enormously effective. But it is no guarantor of order.

2. Diffusion of Economic (and therefore military) Power

Economic power is also dispersing, though less rapidly than is often supposed. America is far less dominant, as has already been noted, than in the 1950s and 1960s. But no new center of power has yet emerged to rival it.

Some countries in East Asia, it is true, have emulated Japan's success in sustaining rapid economic growth over years and even decades, narrowing the gap between their wealth and that of the developed countries; this process of catch-up may be (but only may be) also taking hold in Latin America and Central Europe. This is, however, a recent phenomenon and one concentrated on only a few of the world's 170-or-so countries.

The difficulty with economic power is that it can be compared and defined in different ways: by category of country, by region, and by country, as well as by comparing sheer value of output (GDP), value of output adjusted for differences in purchasing power (so-called purchasing-power-parity GDPs), and wealth measured by GDP per head of population. Several measures are presented in the following charts.

Share of World Output

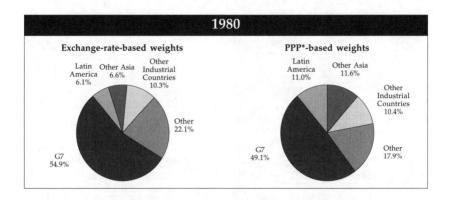

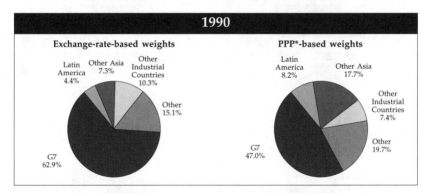

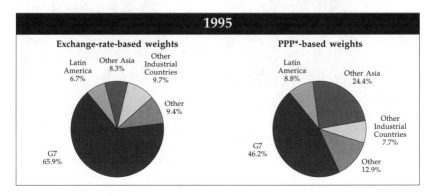

Sources: IMF; World Bank
* Purchasing-power parity

Top 20 Countries

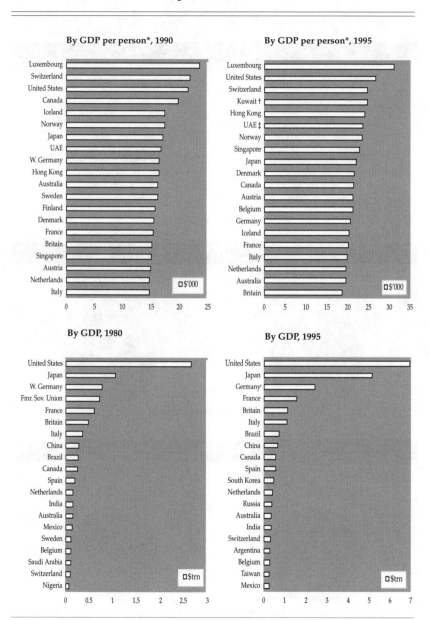

By GDP per person*, 1990

Luxembourg	
Switzerland	
United States	
Canada	
Iceland	
Norway	
Japan	
UAE	
W. Germany	
Hong Kong	
Australia	
Sweden	
Finland	
Denmark	
France	
Britain	
Singapore	
Austria	
Netherlands	
Italy	

□$'000

0 5 10 15 20 25

By GDP per person*, 1995

Luxembourg	
United States	
Switzerland	
Kuwait †	
Hong Kong	
UAE ‡	
Norway	
Singapore	
Japan	
Denmark	
Canada	
Austria	
Belgium	
Germany	
Iceland	
France	
Italy	
Netherlands	
Australia	
Britain	

□$'000

0 5 10 15 20 25 30 35

By GDP, 1980

United States	
Japan	
W. Germany	
Fmr. Sov. Union	
France	
Britain	
Italy	
China	
Brazil	
Canada	
Spain	
Netherlands	
India	
Australia	
Mexico	
Sweden	
Belgium	
Saudi Arabia	
Switzerland	
Nigeria	

□$trn

0 0.5 1 1.5 2 2.5 3

By GDP, 1995

United States	
Japan	
Germany⁰	
France	
Britain	
Italy	
Brazil	
China	
Canada	
Spain	
South Korea	
Netherlands	
Russia	
Australia	
India	
Switzerland	
Argentina	
Belgium	
Taiwan	
Mexico	

□$trn

0 1 2 3 4 5 6 7

Sources: World Bank and OECD for GDP per person in 1990; OECD and ING Barings for GDP per person in 1995; World Bank and EIU for GDP in 1980; OECD and J.P. Morgan for GDP in 1995.
* At purchasing-power parity   † 1994   ‡ 1993   ∞ Net material product

FDI Inflows
($bn)

	1985	1995
European Union	16.1	111.9
North America	21.3	71.4
Other developed	3.4	19.9
Total developed	*40.8*	*203.2*
Africa	2.9	4.7
Latin America	7.3	26.6
Europe	0.0	0.3
Asia	5.3	68.1
Total developing	*15.6*	*99.7*
Central and Eastern Europe	0.0	12.1
Total	*56.5*	*314.9*

Source: UNCTAD

Trade and Output
(1985 = 100)

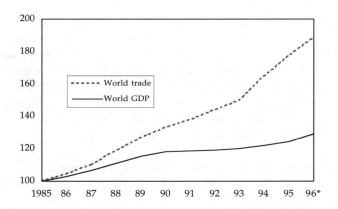

Sources: WTO; IMF
* Estimate

Leaving the detail aside, the main point these comparisons illustrate is that in terms both of raw output and wealth, the world economy remains dominated by the Trilateral countries. Although developing countries, especially in Asia, have grown more rapidly recently, they are doing so from a low base. This low base gives rise to statistical illusion. The extra output associated with 10 percent growth in China's annual GDP ($700 billion) is equivalent to merely a little over 1 percent growth in the United States' annual GDP or 1.9 percent growth in Japan. China's achievements are formidable. But they should be kept in perspective.

Only the purchasing-power-parity measure shows a substantial improvement in the relative position of the developing countries and of Asia (broadly defined but excluding Japan). That is significant, since PPP is a better measure of the ability of countries to turn their income into goods, including military ones, although one must add a statistician's caution on all PPP comparisons: they are indicative rather than strictly accurate, and they become less meaningful the more that a country's internal prices and external exchange rate are artificially (and, in the long term, unsustainably) controlled. That caution applies particularly to China.

In the end, the only valid, general conclusion is this: although the G-7 countries are broadly maintaining their dominant position as a group or as their various regions, a substantial number of individual developing countries, including most notably China, have become considerably wealthier, slightly narrowing the gap between them as individual countries and the G-7 and, probably more significantly, opening up a gap between themselves and some of their neighbors. That increased wealth is undoubtedly to the general benefit, but it also brings with it increased power, firstly in global negotiations or disputes of any kind; secondly in the ability to project military power either regionally or globally. More countries, in other words, are able to have an influence than ever before. And one new economic power has a greater motive, both contemporary and historical, for seeking such influence than do the others: China.

3. Nuclear Proliferation, Amid Technological Dispersal

More countries are also able to obtain the wherewithal to develop, manufacture and deploy weapons of mass destruction than ever before.

This is not directly related to wealth, since nuclear programs are not hugely expensive. Rather, it is the consequence of three changes: the weakening of the discipline imposed on trade in military technology during the Cold War; the collapse of the Soviet Union, leaving nuclear materials in a wide range of hands in the newly independent countries; and the growing trade in waste from nuclear-power stations for re-processing.

It may not be far-fetched, in fact, to suggest that nuclear proliferation is currently arising as a problem in inverse proportion to wealth: as poorer and often totalitarian countries are left behind by economic growth elsewhere, the incentive to make up lost ground in influence or defensive capability by developing a nuclear program appears to increase. So far, that suggestion applies only to North Korea and Iraq. But in the future it may apply more widely. And, as is often remarked upon, it may apply also to terrorist groups.

4. Globalization, by Choice

One consequence of the diffusion of military and economic power, allied with concerns about nuclear proliferation both among countries and among terrorist groups, has been a certain pessimism about the future, as well as a feeling that globalization is an unstoppable movement being imposed upon country after country.

This is a misunderstanding: diffusion of power is the result overwhelmingly of positive changes, not negative ones. And globalization, the formation of a relatively open world economy, is taking place because of the voluntary decisions of governments. Computer and communication technology has, it is true, played a part in encouraging the shift of companies from country to country and the growth of international trade, and might therefore be described as an exogenous force. But this factor is small compared with the two fundamental changes that have taken place: that countries have chosen to be more open to trade and investment flows; and that they are not currently fighting wars against each other. Many of them are thereby becoming richer.

The remarkable thing about the 1990s is that this choice is suddenly available to more countries than ever before. Many are taking it. As such, they are opting for interdependence rather than self-sufficiency, in a bid to improve their welfare through trade, foreign investment, specialization and the international diffusion of knowledge. The Uruguay Round of GATT trade liberalization, concluded in 1994, was remarkable both for the number of countries participating and for the fact that obstacles to liberalization came more in the developed world than in the developing countries, a reversal of the pattern typical in the 1960s and 1970s.

Does this mean that nation-states no longer matter? Emphatically not. Despite all this interdependence, the world is a long way away from a time when the major swings in countries' fortunes are set principally at a global rather than a national level. Mexico's economic crisis in 1994-95 was signalled by cross-border capital flows, but was domestic in origin. Immediately afterwards, some other countries felt the ripple effects of a loss of confidence on the part of international investors in emerging markets. But the effect was short-lived. And, seeking reassurance, international investors compared and contrasted domestic policies in order to decide which countries might be "the next Mexico" and which might not.

It remains overwhelmingly the case that national policies are the key determinants of national economic success. The quality of national education and infrastructure; the ability of national security forces to keep the peace; the willingness of governments to allow private enterprise to develop in a stable macroeconomic and regulatory environment; the extent of state ownership and the proportion of financial flows intermediated by the state: these are the most important factors in determining which countries prosper and which countries wither. "Globalization" does not represent a force imposed upon countries from the outside; joining the world economy, and thus "globalizing" is a conscious policy decision, made at a national level. And as such, the policy decision can also be reversed.

5. Backlash Against Globalization

Despite the many predictions of the end of the nation-state, and of the replacement of national institutions by supranational ones, there is a growing political reaction against this voluntary globalization. It is taking a predominantly local or national form.

The decision to open economies to trade and investment flows always triggers off an adjustment process, as resources move from inefficient, uncompetitive industries to more efficient, competitive ones. Indeed, that transfer is the whole point of the decision to open. But it brings with it losers as well as winners, and so inevitably brings a backlash from the losers. In 1995-97 such a reaction has been seen in the strikes and demonstrations in France against unemployment, budget cuts and welfare reform; it has been seen on the streets of Argentina, in sometimes violent demonstrations; it has been seen in South Korea, in strikes against changes in labor laws; it has been seen and heard in the United States in the speeches and political campaigns of Pat Buchanan and Ross Perot, in France in the campaigns of Jean-Marie Le Pen, and around the world in the new fashion for books and articles decrying free-market capitalism, even from such denizens of global capitalism as George Soros and Sir James Goldsmith.

So far, that backlash has not brought about a serious reversal of the trend towards voluntary globalization. Indeed, thanks particularly to fear of Japanese competition, the 1980s were a worse decade for renewed rich-country protectionism than the 1990s have so far proved, with much wider use of techniques such as "voluntary restraint agreements" and anti-dumping rules to limit imports. At worst, the pressure from losers and from skeptics about freer trade has simply slowed down further progress rather than causing a reversal. But the pressure is there, and could easily grow.

In truth, the effect on jobs and incomes in the rich world of freer global trade is small compared with the effect of technological change (as was shown in the 1996 report to the Trilateral Commission by Robert Z. Lawrence, Yutaka Kosai and Niels Thygesen entitled *Globalization and Trilateral Labor Markets: Evidence and Implications*). Yet trade takes the brunt of the political criticism and pressure. The reasons, presumably, are that trade is something that can readily be affected by public policy, unlike technological change, and that foreigners do not vote in national elections and so are ready scapegoats. So much for the end of the nation-state.

6. Political Instability in Russia and China

The most disordered aspect of the new world order is that neither of the two military powers capable of being a serious rival to America (either actually in the recent past or potentially in the near future) can be said to have a stable political system. Plenty of other important countries look unstable, too: Indonesia, Iraq, Pakistan, South Africa, Egypt, even possibly Mexico, to name but six. But the significance of their instability pales beside that of Russia and China.

Russia has a democracy, but with weak political, legal and judicial institutions. The military is in a state of collapse. For seven months after his re-election as president in June 1996, Boris Yeltsin was in effect absent on sick leave from the Kremlin. His re-election had staved off a victory for his Communist challenger, Gennady Zyuganov, that had looked odds-on at the start of 1996. Now his most popular rival is the decidedly illiberal Alexander Lebed.

China's political institutions look more stable, with no serious threat to the power of the Communist Party. But that appearance is misleading, for China's leadership is in a state of transition. The death on February 19th of Deng Xiaoping, paramount leader since the mid-1970s, is not the beginning of that transition (he played no active role for at least two years before his death), but it could well mark the beginning of some sort of power struggle. Around him Deng built a political structure stronger and more durable than that surrounding Mao Zedong at the time of his death, perhaps, but one that is nevertheless far from immune to challenge. President Jiang Zemin has an established position as Deng's chosen successor, but it is also likely that others will have held back their bids for status until after Deng left the scene. If a power struggle does ensue, it will take place just as China resumes sovereignty over Hong Kong and as Taiwan's independence grows as an issue in domestic Chinese politics and in regional concerns.

In both Russia and China, the consequences of such instability may be purely domestic. But in both cases the consequences could equally well be international, especially as internal power struggles are likely to bring nationalism to the fore.

THE MAIN TASKS FOR THE NEXT TEN YEARS

Those six themes provide the basis on which the future tasks of managing the international system are likely, in the view of this essay's author, to be built. As has already been said, these themes are far from exhaustive. There will never be any shortage of tasks for public policy, either in international affairs or in the running of democratic industrialized societies. The supply of new problems always at least keeps pace with the supply of solutions to old problems. The job of this essay is, however, to set out the priorities and to sketch the general objectives for those concerned with managing the international system.

Put crudely and far too broadly, the basic objective must be to maintain those three simple facts that were described earlier as marking out this century's final decade as being substantially different from the previous 90 years. These are:

- that no substantial country is either at war with another or actively threatening a war;

- that no country currently believes that it can attain dominance over a substantial slice of the globe;

- and that the prevailing tendency virtually throughout the world is to lower national barriers to trade rather than to raise or to preserve them.

Moreover, that objective should be pursued without a fixed notion in mind of how the world will look in 10 years' time, or 25 years' time, or further ahead than that. Nobody knows how the world will look in the future; extrapolations of present trends have no predictive value. And there is a danger of being misled by such predictions into dealing with countries now as if they are already in the condition they are predicted to have in 2010 or 2025, say.

With that broad objective in mind, the most important tasks can be laid out in the following way.

1. Maintaining the Trilateral Alliance

The biggest potential discouragement to any country or group of countries that might in the future seek to dominate a slice of the globe would be the overwhelming strength, and cohesion, of the Trilateral countries. Building that cohesion, and preserving it, ought to be the primary goal of all the Trilateral countries.

Yet this is also the most difficult task of all, given the very absence of threat. Had it not been for the Cold War, and for the hot war in Korea, the Trilateral alliance might never have been formed. But that fact does not make its existence any less valuable. And the present absence of threat makes the alliance more important, not less, since the state of flux in which the world finds itself could readily encourage budding powers to take advantage of any power vacuum that might emerge, as has often been the case in the past.

The principal means by which the alliance must be maintained is by the avoidance of unnecessary and unproductive conflict between the alliance partners. At present, such conflict chiefly takes an economic form: arguments over import barriers, or over competition to promote exports, whether within the Trilateral countries or elsewhere. Trade skirmishes and export battles are far from new, and took place throughout the Cold War. But they are more dangerous now, for two reasons: because of the lack of a common security threat; and because in a backlash against trade or globalization, attacking one's biggest trading partners (i.e., the Trilateral countries) is the easiest, and therefore most politically tempting, way to have a big impact.

Unproductive trade friction has been a particular characteristic of the US-Japan relationship in recent years, reaching its zenith in 1995 with America's threat of a trade war over car parts. The existence of regional powers within Asia, with a potential interest in exploiting any serious division between America and Japan, ought to be sufficient reason to seek to quell any future escalation of trade conflict across the Pacific. Such conflict has not, moreover, been wholly absent in relations between the United States and Europe, or indeed the United States and Canada, most notably over the Helms-Burton act that directs sanctions against European and Canadian companies doing business with Cuba, and over the D'Amato bill which seeks similar measures against non-American companies doing business with Iran and Libya.

The other important source of potential divisions within the alliance will arise from defense, security and sometimes trade policy towards each alliance member's near neighbors. When the EU frames its policy towards Eastern Europe and Russia, when the United States frames its policy towards Latin America and when Japan frames its policy towards China, Indonesia or the Koreas, there is a danger that local needs and interests diverge from the interests and perceptions of more distant partners.

2. Fighting the Domestic Backlash Against Global Liberalism

Unemployment, income inequality, strain on public finances and public services, anti-immigrant agitation, the social ills of conventional crime and drug-related crime: these are the factors likeliest to turn members of the Trilateral alliance against liberal trade and investment, and to make policies inward-looking and unilateralist rather than outward-looking and multilateral.

Such ills are all therefore dangers to the Trilateral alliance itself, as well as being likely, through trade friction or, for example, friction over the drug trade, to bring about tensions with countries outside the Trilateral alliance. They probably pose greater immediate dangers in Western Europe because of the levels of unemployment in France, Germany and their neighbors. But a shift in the economic cycle could well revive such problems in the United States, too. And in Japan a prolongation of the current economic stagnation would pose a risk of higher unemployment, which could endanger that country's relatively liberal instincts, both towards Trilateral allies and towards East Asian neighbors.

3. Dealing with Poverty in Post-Welfare-State Societies

It follows from the danger of a backlash against globalization that the crucial domestic task for industrialized countries will be dealing with the most deep-rooted potential source of that backlash, namely poverty. In the 1960s and 1970s, countries in North America and Western Europe dealt with this issue by building welfare states to varying degrees, using taxpayer-funded income support, health and pension schemes to provide both a safety net and a sense of public obligation towards welfare requirements in general.

This approach is now discredited, for two reasons: because welfare schemes have failed adequately to solve the problems at which they are directed; and, most crucially, because the combination of high unemployment and demographic change mean that the public finances can no longer afford existing levels of entitlement. One of the toughest current tasks of governments all over the world is to cut welfare spending. Yet too often it is being done purely to save money, rather than to readjust priorities and expectations. However much spending is cut, the problems to which welfare states were a solution will remain: poverty, an urban underclass, insecurity in old age, gross inequality in health provision. New solutions will have to be found.

4. Managing the Relationship with Russia

Since the end of the Cold War, security discussion in Europe has naturally been preoccupied with the collapse of the Warsaw Pact and the desire of Central and Eastern European countries to place themselves under the umbrella of NATO. This has, however, given rise to a new worry: the division of Europe between Russia and the West, if not into armed camps then rival spheres of influence. In other words, a "new Yalta." Avoiding such a division, and thus a gulf between Russia and the rest of Europe, must be a key policy aim.

The enlargement of NATO to include Poland, Hungary and the Czech Republic will doubtless go ahead after NATO's special summit in July of this year. Given the promises that have been made already, to abandon enlargement now would be likely not only to damage relations with those countries severely but would also bust the NATO alliance itself.

Beyond that initial enlargement, however, two things need to be recognized. The first is that extending the scope of the European Union into Central and Eastern Europe is a better way to offer help and confidence to countries in those regions, since it is less likely to stoke up Russian fears of expansion towards its borders. EU enlargement will pose large demands on EU institutions and EU cohesion, but such strains should be compared with the fact that enlarging NATO would stretch the credibility of NATO's security guarantee and its operational effectiveness to the breaking point and probably beyond.

The second thing to be recognized is that the priority for the West, before considering further NATO enlargement, must be the establishment of a more stable and secure relationship with Russia itself. This matters not only for the short term, as a means to obtain Russian acquiescence for NATO expansion, but also for the longer term. The need to manage the relationship with Russia is a permanent one.

As well as broader treaties and associations, most crucially in due course with the European Union, the first steps to manage this relationship could include the NATO-Russia council already envisaged, to involve Russia directly in NATO discussions. It can include reworking the treaty on conventional forces in Europe. It can also usefully include a new strategic arms reduction treaty ("START III"), to cut the number of long-range nuclear weapons held by the United States and Russia below the levels (3,000-3,500 apiece) agreed to in "START II," which Congress ratified in 1993 but which still languishes unratified in the Russian Duma.

5. Managing Nuclear Disarmament

START III would be an important source of pressure for wider agreement to reduce the number of nuclear weapons and to secure broader enforcement of anti-proliferation measures. In a world of diffuse power and multifarious sources of potential threat, it would be foolish for the Trilateral countries to switch, as some ex-generals have recently suggested, to a policy of complete nuclear disarmament. Nuclear weapons cannot be disinvented; a world in which the Trilateral countries had no nuclear weapons would be more dangerous, not safer. But having fewer nuclear weapons, with numbers further limited by treaty, would be a desirable aim.

A new, low balance (perhaps of 2,000 weapons each, or fewer) between America and Russia would save money and help to ease the tensions between Russia and the West. It would also strengthen the case for treaty curbs on Chinese, British and French weapons too, and (although the point should not be exaggerated) strengthen the West's moral position with regard to nuclear issues worldwide.

6. Managing the Relationship with China

While Russia is an insecure, shrunken power at risk of harking back to past glories, China is a more secure, growing power at risk of harking back to past humiliation. As was stated earlier, China poses a high risk of political instability. Most of all, however, it is a country re-emerging into regional and world affairs after many years of relative seclusion. That re-emergence offers many opportunities, but also poses challenges and causes tensions both for China and for the outside world.

Much attention has been devoted to extrapolations of China's recent economic growth, to show its likely world prominence in the early decades of the next century. Yet this growth is not inevitable; it could be interrupted by many things, particularly internal political or military conflict or by simple policy mistakes. What is clear in 1997, however, is that given China's development in the past 15 years or more and given the degree of interdependence between China's economy and those of its neighbors and the West, China will pose challenges whether it continues to grow at its recent pace or whether it experiences an economic setback. One way or another, the outside world and China have reason to learn to live with one another.

The sources of tension are well-known: trade friction, caused by the difference between Chinese government and business practices and those typical elsewhere; human rights, made prominent in China by virtue of the country's size, prominence and recent openness to trade and investment; weapons proliferation due to Chinese exports, particularly with regard to those to "rogue" and semi-rogue states such as Iran and Pakistan; and territorial claims in the South China Sea and, of course, over Taiwan.

The solution is also well-known: engaging China in regional and multilateral institutions, such as the Asia-Pacific Economic Cooperation forum and the World Trade Organization. Familiar solutions are not necessarily easy ones, however, nor are they guaranteed to succeed. Not only is China a totalitarian society, it is also, like the United States, a naturally self-centered one that considers that the world revolves around it. Put more gently, China is even less comfortable with the idea of pooling sovereignty through international organizations than is the United States. Even once inside the WTO, for example, China will be a difficult member to manage.

The long-term difficulty with China can be straightforwardly put. East Asia is arguably the one area of the world in which the current power framework remains highly unnatural. What is unnatural about East Asia is that America is overwhelmingly present; China's regional role is overwhelmingly absent; and the Korean peninsula is the last remnant of the Cold War, one that could turn hot at any moment. In this Japan plays a crucial role, even though as a regional power, and potential superpower, its presence too is less than its economic significance might imply. Japan's role is that through the US-Japan security treaty it serves to legitimate America's continued presence in the area. Managing the natural pressure to alter the regional power balance between China and America, while maintaining Japan's linchpin role, will be the long-term task.

7. Nurturing the Multilateral Rule of Law

The final key task, related to virtually all of the preceding six tasks, is to build a multilateral rule of law, and to nurture it. By this is meant principally a set of multilateral rules for trade and investment, through the World Trade Organization, under which the inevitable disputes arising from globalization can be managed. Nurturing and reforming the United Nations, as well as international arms control and anti-proliferation treaties, also fall under this heading.

Globalization is essentially happening as a result of the free choices of national governments, but those governments are thereby substituting domestic rules for international ones. That substitution will be stable and sustainable only as long as those rules are broadly accepted and enforced, and as long as those rules cover a very broad range of trade and investment sectors. The Uruguay Round made great strides in extending the range of sectors covered by such rules, and the range of countries that are subject to the rules. Yet many sectors remain outside the WTO's ambit, particularly in services trade and agriculture. And, most important, the WTO's ability to enforce the rules remains in considerable doubt. The biggest reason for that doubt is the unwillingness of the rich, Trilateral countries, particularly the United States, to accept the WTO, either as a rule-setter or a rule-enforcer. The Helms-Burton act is the latest and greatest threat to the WTO. Even if peace breaks out between the United States, Canada and Europe over Helms-Burton (as is to be hoped), however, there will still be plenty of challenges to it in the future.

The WTO's work is highly technical, and thus either inaccessible to, or tedious for, all but the aficionados. Yet the organization's fate may well hold in its grip the future of this decade's unusual progress in the liberalization of trade and capital flows, and thus the future of globalization itself. Failure to build a multilateral rule of law for trade and investment, where the collective interest in such a system is so clear, will also bode ill for the construction of rules of law in areas in which the individual and the collective interest diverge much more readily, such as environmental agreements and nuclear proliferation.

THE DANGEROUS WEAKNESSES OF
THE TRILATERAL COUNTRIES

Two things, at least, will by now be clear from this essay. The first is that the author considers that the future is defined more by disorder and obscurity than by order and clarity, and that policies must be shaped accordingly to be agile and to deal with a range of potential dangers. The second is that the author considers that the Trilateral alliance has a role to play that is, if anything, even more crucial in this disordered future than it was in the dangerous order of the Cold War.

The motherhood-and-apple-pie conclusion to draw from the above would be that the United States, Canada, the European Union and Japan must work together to build a shared leadership. But such a view would be more pious than practical, revealing little about actual policy or about challenges. A more helpful approach is to concentrate on the weaknesses of each of the Trilateral members, with regard to the tasks and objectives already outlined. Put simply, if cohesion in the Trilateral alliance is identified as the key objective, it is necessary for each member of that alliance to understand the problems that the other members face in maintaining that cohesion. Because of this emphasis on weaknesses liable to endanger the alliance's tasks, Canada is excluded. This author can see no Canadian weaknesses likely to be dangerous.

Japan

This author's view is that in the medium term or beyond, Japan may well face the greatest difficulties in maintaining its position and role inside the alliance. This is not because the present or probable future leadership of Japan, or indeed Japanese public opinion, is likely to desire a break with the alliance. It is because Japan sits on the edge of the region of the world that, at present, looks the most unstable. For that reason, Japan could well be faced with the most difficult strategic dilemmas among the Trilateral members.

Since the American occupation ended in 1951, Japan has based its security policy on the US-Japan alliance and its international economic policy on membership of multilateral institutions. Throughout this period, the principal threat was considered to be the Soviet Union; China was either a subsidiary threat or considered dormant. The US-Japan alliance remains the cornerstone of Japanese security policy, and is the cornerstone too of American policy in Asia. It remains strong. What needs to be recognized by fellow Trilateral members, however, is that changes within Asia are swirling around this alliance and could readily, in the future, start to erode it.

Principal among those changes is the rise of China, and the emergence of a more assertive Chinese attitude towards Taiwan and the South China Sea. Another big change that looks on the cards is some sort of alteration in the shape of power on the Korean peninsula. North Korea is forever assumed, rightly or wrongly, to be on the verge of collapse. South Korea, too, is far from stable, with its first truly democratic government reeling from corruption scandals and from strikes and protests. These troubles in the South may prove short-lived. But the peninsula as a whole has the clear potential to produce major upsets in the power balance, peace and stability of the region. It is on Japan's doorstep, and something like 600,000 Koreans live in Japan, with family ties to either the North or the South. Not only that, it is also home to one of America's last remaining forward deployments of troops.

There are plenty of other ways in which Asia could prove unstable, but China and Korea are the two that could pose the greatest challenges for Japan. A natural aim for a pugnacious Chinese leadership would be to seek to break Japan's links with America. A natural consequence of bloodshed on the Korean peninsula would be to force the Japanese finally to choose between being pacifists and being truly engaged, in military terms, overseas.

Meanwhile, Japan is undergoing a wrenching restructuring of its economy and, quite possibly, of its governmental system too. Economic stagnation and financial-market slump over the past five years have challenged the political system in new ways and have brought to light deep-seated problems within government of corruption, excessive discretionary power and lack of accountability. A smooth adjustment to these challenges is possible, especially given the currently low level of unemployment, and thus lack of social pressures, enjoyed by Japan. But it is also possible that these challenges could send Japanese politics, and public opinion, in wholly new directions if frustration grows and if external shocks intervene.

One of those directions, which cannot be called probable but is certainly conceivable, could be a swing of public and political opinion against the United States and towards a more Asian approach. The strength of local opinion has already been shown in Okinawa in the protests in 1996 against the American bases on the island. For the moment, that is clearly an isolated case. But things could change, especially if Japan is put under pressure, either by the United States or by events in Asia. "The Japan that can say No" may have been a book by a maverick politician, Shintaro Ishihara, but it nevertheless struck something of a chord. The current prime minister, Ryutaro Hashimoto, gained popularity as trade minister by standing up to America in the 1995 trade dispute over cars.

The worst mistake, with Japan, would be to take it for granted. The second worst would be to ignore the regional pressures under which it is liable to find itself.

The European Union

Currently, Western Europe faces the biggest domestic difficulties among the Trilateral partners. It has the highest levels of unemployment, and the toughest task in reforming welfare states and public finances. Those are its principal weaknesses within the alliance. The European Union continues to be the region where the dangers of a backlash against open trade and investment are the greatest. But there is also a secondary weakness that must be taken into account. This is that the yearning for an independent European voice, in foreign and security policy as well as trade, defined by its ability to be independent of the United States, remains strong.

The EU has proved frustratingly slow to adjust to the two big changes that have taken place on its landmass. The first, the unification of Germany, led Helmut Kohl and others to seek a greater integration of the EU to compensate for Germany's potentially increased power. But there are also forces pushing in the opposite direction, suggesting that a larger and more self-centered Germany might lead the EU to a looser, more confederal structure than the Maastricht treaty appeared to envisage. The battle is being argued out over the plan for EMU, Economic and Monetary Union. The second big change, the emergence of new, democratic market economies in Central and Eastern Europe, freed by the end of the Cold War, poses the challenge of enlargement and, again, a looser, less centrally ambitious Europe. This the EU has barely begun to come to grips with, because of its own constitutional debate and because of the difficulty of adapting existing policies, most notoriously the Common Agricultural Policy, to new entrants.

These weaknesses are liable to make the EU a sometimes baffling, sometimes irritating, often frustrating partner. Yet they should not be overblown. In fundamental terms, the EU does not have a viable alternative strategy to the alliance. It may cavil at it, and seek an independent voice, but it does not look likely to be pulled in any new direction in the foreseeable future. While Japan has to contend with, and possibly accommodate itself to, a stronger China, the EU's main strategic worry is a weak, fissiparous Russia.

The EU's sluggishness in making up its mind what, exactly, it wants to be reflects the complexity of its task as well as the fact that treaty-based institutions are especially difficult to reform and re-direct. The main concern arising from that sluggishness is that EU expansion is moving far more slowly than NATO expansion, which could give rise to even greater pressure later for further expansion of the military alliance rather than the EU itself.

The consequences of unemployment are hard to assess. Currently, although extremist parties have grown in strength in recent years, they remain small. The European economies, with their high-quality education systems and infrastructure, are stronger than they sometimes seem. Forecast growth rates for France and Germany in 1997 are, for instance, very similar to those for the United States, which is these days heralded as the world's strongest economy. Forecasts are not facts, admittedly, but Europe's problems should nevertheless not be exaggerated. The EU's basic problem is not economic sloth as such, but rather an apparently structurally high level of unemployment. Solving that will require painful domestic reforms to labor and product markets.

This may make European politicians more sensitive about trade policy and thus globalization, but it is likelier that the focus of dissent and dispute will be internal rather than external. Britain's high unemployment and bitter strikes over labor market reforms in the 1980s had no evident external impact. The same could well prove true in Europe as a whole. The real questions about the EU revolve around whether it will become riven by internal arguments, not around its policy towards its Trilateral partners.

The United States
The United States can fairly be described as the hub of the Trilateral alliance, even at the risk of mixing the Trilateral metaphor. As such, its greatest weakness has always been, and will always be, the self-centered nature of its politics. All nation-states are self-centered, in one

way or another, and all pass through periods of introspection. This essay has already suggested that both Japan and the EU are passing through just such periods. So why make this point about the United States?

The reason is that the United States is, as was observed earlier, more akin to China in its self-centeredness than to Japan or the EU. The self-centeredness of Japan and the EU is tempered by these countries' sense of their own vulnerability. America, by contrast, by virtue of its size and its power, can see itself as the "middle kingdom," in the Chinese phrase, around which the rest of the world revolves. Self-centered policies by the United States have a high chance (or risk, depending on your point of view) of success. That makes them especially tempting.

Debates in the United States over foreign policy, in the broadest sense, can frequently be characterized as arguments between those advocating a self-centered approach and those favoring a broader good. The broader camp often wins, particularly in security matters. But the tussle is there and the self-centered camp also can score victories to its name, especially when commerce is involved. One recent one was the Helms-Burton act, which is giving rise to a challenge to another main arena for this tussle, the World Trade Organization. The self-centered camp cannot accept the pooling of sovereignty implied by membership of the WTO, or indeed of other multilateral organizations including the United Nations.

This force within US politics is much stronger and broader than the explicitly protectionist and xenophobic tendency exemplified by Patrick Buchanan and Ross Perot. It crosses party lines within Congress, and has a wide national base. Although this force has always existed, three related factors have recently increased its strength: the end of the Cold War, and hence of the clarity of the need for alliances with Europe and Japan; the rise of the idea that economic competition is now the main arena of international affairs; and, most recently, a sudden revival in confidence about the American economy and American technology, which seems to be producing a superiority complex.

The importance of this weakness cannot be over-stated. If unchecked, it is liable to make the United States a constant source of challenge to the multilateral rules of law that a globalized economy requires, and to lead it to undermine multilateral peacekeeping and security institutions. It is liable also to lead the United States to confront its partners at least as often as its potential enemies, and thus to risk undermining the cohesion of its own alliances.

There are also strong grounds for optimism, however. They lie, fundamentally, in the broad and powerful countervailing force against such self-centeredness that exists within the United States itself, deriving from the people and the arguments that have given the United States the leadership role that it now holds. Nevertheless America's Trilateral partners must recognize this weakness of self-centeredness, and give those people and those arguments all possible support.

*   *   *

The world that has emerged in the 1990s is one of great promise and of great opportunity. To put that promise and that opportunity in danger by weakening the Trilateral alliance would be folly, grand scale. The position of the Trilateral alliance should be that we must concentrate on making ourselves a strong coalition, but an open coalition—open to the rest of the world, open to the desire of other countries to share our values and to drive forward in the same direction. A strong coalition and an open coalition is necessary to have the agility to deal with the unpredictable nature of the next ten years, and of the future at any stage.

JAPAN IN NEED OF REFORM AND TRILATERALISM

Koji Watanabe

More than twenty years have passed since Japan joined the Group of Seven (G-7) summit in Rambouillet. For Japan, participation was understood as official recognition of its becoming a major industrial democracy. The earlier establishment of the Trilateral Commission among North America, Western Europe, and Japan also symbolized its acceptance as an equal.

Now, Japan finds itself in trouble. The political, administrative, and economic system that enabled its development for the half century since the end of World War II has ceased to function well. Everybody, regardless of his or her political party or economic or social group, has started emphasizing the importance of reform. Yet no clear-cut image of this reform has emerged so far.

Considering this domestic setting, does Trilateral cooperation still benefit Japan? This essay attempts to answer this question by, first, elaborating on the nature of the problems and on how the Trilateral exercise can be of help in concrete terms and, second, presenting a Japanese perspective on Trilateralism in general.

JAPAN IN NEED OF REFORM

National Goals Have Been Achieved

At the risk of making a gross generalization, one can assert that the Japanese are not unhappy about the present life in Japan, but they are uneasy about the future. This general frame of mind of the Japanese is related to the perceived fact that two national goals have been attained: "growth" (by catching up with the United States) and "democracy" (by creating a rich egalitarian society through the protection of the weak).

The following facts illustrate this:

- The 1994 per capita GNP, US$34,630, was among the highest in the world in dollar terms, second only to Luxembourg and Switzerland. By 1990, Japan's labor productivity (per capita GNP measured with purchasing-power-parity exchange rates) had more or less caught up with that of the United States.

- Aggregate financial assets of Japanese households are estimated at 1,200 trillion yen (US$10 trillion, based on US$1=120 yen).

- The unemployment rate is getting higher, but at 3.4 percent it is still the lowest among industrial democracies, if not in the world.

- In terms of crime, Japan is among the safest countries to live in, and environmental problems are under control.

- Japan has been the largest donor of economic assistance to developing countries for five consecutive years, with US$14.5 billion for 1995.

Juxtaposed with the good news above, however, is the bad news:

- Since 1992, the Japanese economy has registered a "strikingly exceptionally low growth rate" (OECD), in spite of huge fiscal stimuli in the form of public works expenditures and special tax reductions.

- The psychological and balance-sheet effect of the bursting of the bubble persists, with the Tokyo Nikkei average hovering around half the level of its peak in 1989.

- The Japanese budget deficit and national debt are among the worst among major industrial democracies, rapidly approaching those of Italy. Japan could not meet the Maastricht EMU criteria for ratio of deficit to GDP or amount of debt relative to GDP.

- Japanese manufacturing firms are shifting production sites abroad, giving rise to fears of "hollowing out." Though the value of overseas production of Japanese manufacturers is 8 percent of total production, compared to 20 percent for the United States, Japan is unique in that high-productivity sectors are moving abroad rather than low-productivity sectors.

- The Japanese population is aging, faster than in other industrial countries. Particularly to be noted is the fact that the total fertility rate (births per woman) is 1.4, which is among the lowest in the world and seems to be falling further.

- By 2010 to 2015, a quarter of the population will be sixty-five years of age or older and every two Japanese in the working population (those fifteen to sixty-four) will have to support one person of sixty-five years or older. In 2011, Japan's population will start to decline.

Bureaucracy in Question

This bad news seems to reflect the fact that the socioeconomic system, which has been centered on attaining the two national goals of catching up to the West and establishing an egalitarian society, has in a sense served its purposes, ceasing to function effectively in a set of new circumstances.

There are different views as to what extent and in what manner bureaucracy has contributed to the high-speed development of the Japanese economy. In fact, one can assert that "bureaucracts did not make Japan great...stable government and, in particular, stable macroeconomic policy did provide an excellent environment for growth, as did the state-led investment in Japan's superb education system" (Bill Emmott, *Kanryo no Daizai* [The Bureaucrats' Deadly Sins], 1996). Clearly, the entrepreneurship of business leaders and the industriousness of workers have played a critical role in carrying out high-speed growth.

Bureaucracy in Japan, however, has played a distinct role in contributing to political stability under the Liberal Democratic Party (LDP) regime, which lasted thirty-eight years until 1993. For one thing, the prevailing perception has long been that the Japanese bureaucracy is well-informed, capable and hard-working, and dedicated to performing state functions. It is generally believed that bureaucracy formulates and executes state functions on behalf of the politicians. The high degree of confidence in the bureaucracy's ability to manage state affairs has been a factor of great significance for political stability.

In reality, during the latter half of the 1970s, a period in which the negative effects and distortions of high-speed growth manifested themselves, the central policy issues became social welfare rather economic ones—such as environmental pollution, distribution of income, social security, and how to fill the gap between growth and welfare. Emphasis shifted from efficiency to distribution, from competition to regulations, from market functions to government (Economic White Paper, 1996).

LDP politics from the early 1980s started taking on an extraordinary role in implementing policies through various ministries guided by the influence of the *zoku* (special interest) Diet members, like the agriculture *zoku* or construction *zoku*. The office of prime minister, who traditionally was head of the LDP, lacked the power to sacrifice or antagonize any important political vested interest of the *zoku*, be it agriculture, construction, postal and telecommunications services, or defense.

The annual allocation of the increased public works budget for fiscal stimulus purposes has been fixed in terms of percentage among the Ministries of Construction, Agriculture, and Transportation, as no prime minister so far has been able to shift the ratio to any sizable degree. In the same vein, when budget or personnel reductions are in order, the method is across-the-board reduction so that no sectors or ministries feel penalized, with specific exceptions to be stipulated, such as defense, science and technology, overseas development assistance (ODA), and energy.

Bureaucracy thus has played a distinct role in protecting and promoting the interests of low-productivity sectors of the economy, a role serving the interests of the LDP since low-productivity sectors (agriculture, construction, and distribution in terms of sectors and small and medium-size enterprises in general) are important voting blocs in Japan. At the same time, those bureaucrats protecting the weak have been proud of their task as upholders of social justice, a sense of mission analogous, in a unique manner, to that of European social democrats. It is to be noted, however, that the Japanese method of protecting the weak and the low-productivity sectors is through protection of producers, rather than through the social security safety net, which is the main method of the European social democrats. This system prevents needed changes in policy emphasis and resource allocations.

Reform and Deregulation

That the buzzword in the October 1996 Diet election was "administrative reform," regardless of political party, reflects the fact that the socioeconomic system that has supported Japanese growth and stability is considered to be in trouble and in need of change. In fact, waves of globalization have started washing Japanese shores relentlessly, challenging the very foundation of the Japanese system.

Japan's industrial structure, which developed in the catch-up phase, is characterized by the juxtaposition of high- and low-productivity sectors. The former is represented by rapidly expanding export industries like automobiles, electronics, and machine tools and the latter by regulated or protected sectors like agriculture, banking, and real estate as well as by nontradable sectors like distribution, construction, transportation, communications, and utilities. The appreciation of the yen was the result of a dramatic expansion of exports from high-productivity sectors whose productivity kept rising, while the productivity of low-productivity and nontradable sectors lagged behind, widening the gap of productivity between the two. Thus, price differentials between domestic and overseas markets became a most salient contradiction of the Japanese economy. In the face of constant pressure for yen appreciation, Japanese manufacturers started shifting a significant portion of their production capacity abroad, particularly to the newly industrializing countries, the member countries of the Association of Southeast Asian Nations (ASEAN), and China. The point they assert is that cost differentials, particularly wage differentials, are too much.

Suddenly, the Japanese have started to realize that the moment they have caught up with the advanced West, East Asia is chasing them in some strategic industries—Korea in semiconductors and iron and steel, Taiwan in electronics and petrochemicals, China in electronic equipment, and Singapore in research and development in general. Not only that, the Japanese have been struck by the fact that the moment they thought they had caught up, the United States seems to be forging ahead to enhance its economic strength. Microsoft leads in the high-tech software industry. The US President and Congress appear intent on reaching budget equilibrium by 2002. Europe is also in the process of reform, with the European Union member states endeavoring to regain fiscal discipline in order to form the European Economic and Monetary Union.

It is in this international economic context that the issues of reform and deregulation in Japan are evolving. The aim is to re-enhance the strength and vitality of the Japanese economy and to change the Japanese system for that purpose. First and foremost, emphasis should be placed on deregulation and, more broadly, on how to redefine the function of the state and the means to carry out such a redefined function. Inevitably, the role of the bureaucracy is at issue, and so is its accountability.

Aging Population

Like a gathering cloud, the aging population poses another challenge for the Japanese system. The aging population will affect the holy trinity of Japanese corporate governance—namely, lifetime employment, seniority wage scales, and company-wide labor unions—which commands the allegiance of company workers. With the decreasing number of fresh graduates, seniority wage scales cannot be maintained in their strict form, and the restructuring of companies as well as reform of the system will inevitably involve shifts and reductions in the work force. Both these factors will severely affect the lifetime employment regime.

The aging population poses a serious problem to the Japanese government budget system, which is also in need of drastic reform due to the mounting deficit and accelerating debt burden. The bond-dependency ratio (government bond issues as a proportion of total expenditure) in the FY1996 budget rose to 28 percent from 10.6 percent in FY1990, and the total government debt to GDP ratio rose to 64.4 percent from 45.6 percent. Both ratios are the highest among the Group of Seven countries, except Italy, and would disqualify Japan in relation to the Maastricht EMU criteria. The rapid deterioration of fiscal conditions in the past five years makes Japanese fiscal reform a matter of great urgency. The Japanese old-age pension system, which depends substantially on fiscal support, will probably become a subject of very serious political debate, in view of the rapidly aging population as well as budgetary constraints.

External Implications of Reform

The critical question concerning Japan and Trilateralism is whether Japan can afford to play an increasingly active international role in the face of multiple challenges that need to be met in reforming the domestic socioeconomic system. Is Trilateralism relevant in this context? Some Japanese might say, "We are preoccupied with mending our own house, so don't bother us," or "We cannot afford internationalism in terms of either intellectual or financial resources."

The process of reform and deregulation will be painful and politically costly. As stated before, since the Japanese system has developed a built-in mechanism protecting the weak sectors of the economy from market competition, a wide range of vested interests are benefiting from the current regulatory system. Various political forces will resist reform and deregulation, and to the extent that reform and deregulation are considered to be linked with foreign interests, there is always the danger of a nationalistic reaction. One can only recall the intense sense of dissatisfaction with and anxiety about the American negotiating style seeking to force the Japanese market open in certain areas.

However, if one analyzes the nature of the challenges and proper ways to meet them, it is obvious that Japan has to be all the more international, all the more engaged and active in the shaping of the international setting within which domestic reform has to take place. Reform must be carried out, not because of foreign pressures, but because without undergoing it, the Japanese economy will lose its vitality and remain stagnant. Without reform, forces of globalization would bypass Japan and make other countries the center of a dynamic Asia.

A case in point is the financial sector and the Japanese version of the "Big Bang," which is planned to be completed by 2001. The Japanese finance sector has been so overregulated that it is losing competitiveness. The so-called convoy system divided the banking, securities, and insurance sectors into air-tight compartments, and the banking sector is further divided into various categories. Fees, commissions, and interest rates are all stipulated in such a way as to protect the weaker institutions; financial authorities protect and guide their activities in detail to insure what is called financial stability. As a result, Tokyo is rapidly losing ground to London, New York, and Frankfurt as a financial center. It is reported that this hollowing out of Tokyo's financial market is due to the web of regulations, various tax burdens, and the high costs of Tokyo.

Unless drastic deregulation in the form of a "Big Bang" is carried out, both Japanese and foreign money would shift away from Japan. Despite Japan's enormous wealth, Shanghai or Singapore might enjoy the status of the principal money center of Asia.

Reform or deregulation is critical, therefore, even in those sectors traditionally considered to be nontradable sectors. In all likelihood, Japan of all industrial democracies is the most in need of reform and deregulation because of the unique role that the government and bureaucracy have played in economic activities. However, the degree of liberalization industrial democracies should carry out must be studied, and the type of regulations most justifiable on certain grounds, like safety and health, should be sorted out. It might be useful for a Trilateral study team to explore the feasibility, cost-effectiveness, and advisability of comprehensive deregulation among advanced industrial countries.

In more general terms, it would be useful to jointly study the role of the state and bureaucracy in the age of globalization. This involves the history, political culture, and political systems of the countries concerned and is a subject of political sensitivity. However, for Japan it might be a useful exercise since never before has the role of the bureaucracy been exposed to such intense criticism.

Another subject that a Trilateral study team might usefully consider is how to manage problems of an aging population. As stated above, Japan has to tackle this intractable problem as a matter of utmost importance. Japan can share the wisdom and insight developed in other countries, while others could benefit from the Japanese experience. While there seems to be little room for taking joint action due to the nature of the issue, there might emerge some sort of formula that can serve as a valuable keyboard for tackling the various problems of an aging society.

THE CHALLENGE FOR TRILATERALISM: A JAPANESE PERSPECTIVE

The concept of Trilateralism is to promote cooperation among the industrial democracies for peace and development of the world. At its origin in the early 1970s was the change in the relative strength of the United States with the rise of Japan and Western Europe in the 1960s. The world then was marked by a strong East-West political divide and a North-South economic divide.

In spite of Sino-Soviet rivalries and the emergence of OPEC countries, the essential twofold divides persisted throughout the 1970s and 1980s. In the 1990s, the East-West divide disappeared at the end of the Cold War and the collapse of the Soviet Union, and the North-South divide became fuzzy with the rapid rise of some of the developing countries, particularly those in East Asia. China by itself is becoming a power center. How do these circumstances affect the validity of Trilateralism?

In Japan's cumulative experience of cooperation with the advanced industrial democracies, the concept of Trilateralism has become ingrained in Japanese management of public affairs. The annual meeting of the G-7 summit has become the most important agenda for Japanese diplomacy, as it represents an indispensable consultative forum among the leaders of the advanced industrial democracies. Indeed, Japan has defined its basic international position as "being a member of free democratic nations sharing common political and economic ideals," as well as "being a country in the Asia Pacific region with close geographic, historical, and cultural bonds [to other countries in the region]" (Diplomatic Bluebook, 1986). Trilateralism has been a natural corollary of these two pillars of Japan's diplomatic identity.

Theoretically, Trilateralism has value because it is a threesome. In the management of Japan-US relations, particularly in negotiating with the United States on a number of issues, especially economic ones, Japan can benefit from the presence of a third party with common values. An objective European view can help check US negotiating pressure if it is injudicious or unreasonable. If, on the other hand, the US position is reasonable and the Europeans agree with it, the situation can be regarded not as US pressure but as benign peer pressure.

Due to the weakness of the Japan-Europe link of the Trilateral relationship, Europe has not fully played its benign third-party role. This is all the more reason to work toward strengthening the link.

A new relevance for Trilateralism might be found in the context of multiple regional or biregional integration processes. In parallel with the Uruguay Round negotiations, which were for the most part an intra-Trilateral process, the North American Free Trade Agreement (NAFTA) and the Asia-Pacific Economic Cooperation (APEC) forum were born and the Asia-Europe Meeting (ASEM) was launched.

The Japanese penchant has been for globalism; hence Japan has become the only advanced industrial country not to be a member of any regional integration scheme, with the exception of APEC. This is due to the negative memory of the trading blocs of the 1930s and to Japan's belief that Japanese economic interests are best served by an expanding global market. With regard to APEC, Japan is one of its strongest proponents for openness. The growth of institutions within single regions (NAFTA or EU) or of institutions including two but not all three Trilateral regions (APEC and ASEM) seems to be compatible with and supportive of Trilateralism. But as a preventive for the emergence of any rivalry among these groupings, the Trilateral process of consultation takes on added importance.

In the early 1990s, after Prime Minister Mahathir of Malaysia proposed the establishment of an East Asian Economic Caucus (in November 1990), the idea of a re-Asianization of Japan found considerable support among Japan's policy establishment because of the growing importance of East Asia for Japan and because of Japan's weariness with the United States. The inclination toward Asia was to a considerable extent a product of negative images of the United States—Japan-bashing, a high-handed negotiating style, unilateralism, unreasonable demands such as numerical targets, the perception that the country was in decline, America's triple deficits and loss of competitiveness. Today, however, while Japanese business interests in the Asian economy, be it in ASEAN countries or China, are still very strong and the shift of production sites will continue on the assumption that appreciation of the yen will resume, enthusiasm for an East Asian community, which is implicitly based on so-called

Asian values, has somewhat subsided. This probably reflects two factors. First, with the big trade issues having been resolved without substantial concessions on Japan's part, the Japanese image of the United States has improved. Second, it became clear that the negative legacy of history still persists—for example, in the form of repeated demands by other Asian countries for apologies about the Pacific War—and that the definition of "Asian values" or the "Asian heart" is elusive.

Against this background, the APEC concept has been promoted to institutionalize regional cooperation encompassing the Pacific Rim nations and to start to take concrete steps to plan integration on the basis of an open, liberal orientation. Japan came to believe that APEC would serve Japanese interests well, since it would not only enhance the mutual integration of Asia and North America but also serve to assure an American presence in Asia.

The formation of ASEM probably greatly satisfies Japan's desire to be a part of both Asia and the West. By joining ASEM, Japan can associate itself with its East Asian partners, and through ASEM, Japan-Europe relations, the weakest leg of Trilateralism, can hopefully be strengthened.

A task of the highest diplomatic priority for Japan is how to work out its relations with China on the basis of mutual respect. That China has been the largest recipient of Japanese ODA attests to the importance Japan attaches to its large neighbor. China is also the second largest trade partner for Japan, after the United States. Negative historical legacies—China's ostensible fear of a revival of Japanese militarism, the Senkaku disputes, and the so-called Taiwan issue—all make Sino-Japanese relations less than satisfactory, however.

In view of the likelihood of China's emergence as a "comprehensive power" with both military and economic power, questions as to how to engage a China that is "territorially amorphous, economically dynamic, culturally proud, socially unstable, [and] politically unsettled" (Yoichi Funabashi, Michel Oksenberg and Heinrich Weiss, *An Emerging China in a World of Interdependence,* 1994) must be addressed not only by Japan or the United States but in a concerted fashion by all Trilateral regions.

For a long time, the Soviet Union was always among the top concerns for the Trilateral partners in terms of East-West relations, and Russia as its core successor is still a subject of common interest and concern, both because of its potential power and because it spreads from Europe to Asia. Japan has an important interest in seeing a stable and prosperous Russia emerge out of the former Soviet Union. The development of the Far East and East Siberia, including Sakhalin Island, will probably increasingly become an interest of the two countries, and the input of Japan's Trilateral partners as well as other Asian countries is welcome. There is no question that NATO expansion concerns Russia; it will concern Japan, too, if it causes a basic shift in the Russian attitude toward the West. As a Trilateral partner, Japan should at least be kept informed of developments.

One of the assumptions of this paper is that it follows the traditional definition of Trilateralism. Trilateralism is the enhancement of a cooperative relationship among advanced industrial democracies which share the common values of basic human rights, democracy, and a market economy and share the responsibility for peace and prosperity of the world because of their degree of influence, either positive or negative, by virtue of their strength. It is to be noted that during the Cold War period, sharing democratic values was automatically interpreted as the legitimate criteria for involvement in Trilateral cooperation. The Cold War is over, and a number of non-Western countries, particularly those of East Asia, are advancing and doing so rapidly with regimes that are democratized to varying degrees.

There are arguments that Trilateralism should be defined as cooperative relations not among North America, Western Europe, and Japan, but among North America, Western Europe, and East Asia, three regions of economic strength. It is anomalous for Japan alone to represent East Asia while Europe is represented by a large number of countries and North America by all geographical members.

However, in spite of these arguments, which should be fully accommodated through practical arrangements, there are sufficient grounds to abide by the present definition of Trilateralism—that is, cooperation among industrial democracies—in view of the fact that there exist many issues of common interest to countries sharing democratic values, market economy, and globalism. But if we are to uphold Trilateral relations in the way we have in the past, namely, Western Europe, North America, and Japan, the binding notion should be that of advanced industrial democracies, not Western civilization. When Japan identified itself as a member of the West, the West meant the West in the sense of East-West divide, not Western civilization. The assumption naturally was that democracy exists outside Western civilization and would prevail because it is the least defective and dangerous system to mankind.

To argue that democracy can take form only in Western civilization is false. We should perhaps remind ourselves that democracy—defined as government of the people, by the people, and for the people—is of relatively recent origin and is still developing. Otherwise, it would be difficult to explain what transpired within Western civilization in Germany, Italy, Spain, or Portugal in the 1930s and 1940s, or in Japan in the same period.

If those who believe that the clash of civilizations is the major source of conflict preach the strengthening of unity among two parties across the Atlantic to form an exclusive bloc, their belief threatens to become a self-fulfilling prophecy by dividing the world by civilization and bringing about the demise of globalism, which many of us have considered one of the cardinal tenets of Western idealism, one which many non-Westerners wish to share. To preach the Trans-Atlantic Free Trade Agreement and creation of a North Atlantic economic organization as a counterpart to NATO in the immediate aftermath of the establishment of the World Trade Organization is a human tragi-irony, and to expand NATO to cover only and all those countries belonging to Western civilization is an attempt to deny the universal nature of democracy when democracy is spreading as never before in one form or another.

EPILOGUE

For someone like myself who has been away from Japan for five years, the change in Japan's self-image as well as in the reality of the Japanese situation is shocking. Five years ago, the Japanese economy was considered strong—in fact, too strong. It was said that the Japanese should not continue to win mah-jong games or their partners would sooner or later stop playing with them. Japanese politics was considered stable, to the point that the permanency of LDP rule was discussed. Today, however, the bubble economy has burst, stock prices have halved, the yen has appreciated, the budget deficit is burgeoning, and the perception of stagnation is pervasive.

This essay is the product of my hurried catch-up with the current mood and reality of what might be called Japan's pessimism. It is possible that I have overemphasized negativism, underestimating the resilience and reboundability of Japanese society. There are some signs that deregulation might be realized on a larger scale than was evident at the time of the Diet elections last autumn.

The concrete proposals for deregulation covering six sectors —finance, physical distribution, advanced telecommunications, land and housing, employment and labor, and medical care and welfare—presented by a small group of professor-experts in a December 1996 report titled "Structural Reform in Six Areas" have been accepted by various ministries and agencies concerned to an extent hardly considered likely last autumn. Why? According to those who have been involved in organizing this exercise, the mood of the public as well as of the establishment has forced the elite bureaucracy to commit to substantive deregulation in spite of the prospect of its turf being stripped away. Bureaucrats may be feeling a positive sense of alarm that if they do not act for reform their positions are in danger in the eyes of the public.

The positive role of scholar-experts in producing the proposals for deregulation was unique in that they were told to present drastic and substantive proposals without consulting the bureaucracy, a method different from various previous advisory councils composed of ex-bureaucrats, people from interested groups, and scholar-experts.

These and other signs give rise to a certain degree of confidence in the economic strength of Japan in the future. Optimists, a rare species nowadays, might say that the history of Japanese economic development has been one of Japanese responses to both internal and external challenges—the devastation of the war, inflation, import liberalization, capital liberalization, two oil shocks. While the challenge of deregulation and reform is a systemic one, the diligence and ingenuity of the people can cope with the challenge, the optimists assert. It may well be, as President Franklin Delano Roosevelt said, "There is nothing to fear but fear itself."

Because of the daunting task of comprehensive deregulation and reform that will last well into the next century, Japan needs a peaceful international environment. For Japan, Asia's future, therefore, has to be an optimistic one. To draw that optimistic picture of Asia, Japan should play a major role within multilayer networks of bilateral, regional, and functional cooperation, of which Trilateralism will continue to form an important pillar upholding the common values of freedom, democracy, and globalism.

MANAGING OUR WAY TO A PEACEFUL CENTURY

Paul Wolfowitz

THE WORLD VIEWED FROM HOME

> The issues are global, and so interlocked, that to consider the problems of one sector oblivious to those of another is but to court disaster for the whole. While Asia is commonly referred to as the gateway to Europe, it is no less true that Europe is the gateway to Asia, and the broad influence of the one cannot fail to have its impact upon the other.

These words do not come from a declaration from some early meeting of the Trilateral Commission. They are the words of General Douglas MacArthur from his famous farewell address to a joint session of the United States Congress nearly forty-six years ago. They are a striking statement of the importance of global interdependence from a very hard-headed strategic thinker.

Unfortunately, they also express a view that seems increasingly unfashionable as publics in the developed democracies become more and more comfortable with the shape of the post-Cold War world. Although there are conflicts aplenty in Bosnia, in Iraq, in Rwanda or in any number of other places around the world, the reaction in most of the advanced countries—except for fitful surges of humanitarian concern—is that fights between Serbs and Bosnians, or Kurds and Iraqis, or Hutus and Tutsis, are no real concern of ours. The attitude is not that expressed in MacArthur's words but something more akin to Neville Chamberlain's lament about being involved in a "quarrel in a faraway country between people about whom we know nothing."

This attitude was reflected during the last Presidential election campaign in the United States by the absence of almost any discussion of foreign policy. Indeed, during the second Presidential debate in San Diego, the questions from the audience—a scientifically selected sample of undecided voters—had so systematically avoided foreign policy that the frustrated moderator, Jim Lehrer, was forced to ask for questions on the subject. The questioner he called on dutifully asked about US-Japan trade policy differences. That was the end of any discussion of foreign policy in that debate, or for that matter in the campaign itself.

This tendency to think that foreign policy no longer matters, and that if it matters at all it is largely just a matter of trade policy, is not unique to the United States and is not without a certain justification. The world is a much safer place for the United States and for American interests than it was during the Cold War. The threats to American interests remain relatively small and remote. The United States is at peace, and to most Americans the threats to that peace seem distant, if not rather contrived.

It is the contention of this essay that the stakes are, to the contrary, very large. The world faces a choice not unlike the one it faced at the end of the last century. Depending on how we make that choice, the next century could bring unprecedented peace among the major powers, new-found prosperity for hundreds of millions of poor people, and a great expansion of democracy and individual freedom. But if we manage badly, the next century could eclipse the twentieth as the bloodiest century in human history.

THE WORLD HEADING INTO
THE TWENTY-FIRST CENTURY

Perhaps the single most important phenomenon of our time is the creation of wealth on a scale and at a pace that are unprecedented in history. The increasingly widespread acceptance of market economic principles, the revolution in information technology, and the advances in productivity made possible by the mobility of goods and capital on a global scale have produced unprecedented productivity gains in many of the world's economies, in some cases exceeding five percent per year on a sustained basis.

This extraordinary wealth creation is lifting hundreds of millions of people out of poverty and creating vast new opportunities for global trade. It has also led to the emergence of a large middle class in a number of countries that previously had none; that, in turn, is at least partly responsible for the triumph of democracy in country after country, including some with no previous history of democratic rule. President Clinton was not exaggerating when he said, in his Second

Inaugural Address, "It is our great good fortune that time and chance have put us not only on the edge of a new century...but on the edge of a bright new prospect in human affairs."

Yet while there seem to be great vistas opening before us, it is worth remembering that the end of the last century was similarly a period of exceptional economic growth and great technological progress which generated great hopes for the coming century. The sustained and significant increases in productivity of industrialized countries beginning in the latter part of the 19th century have been called "one of the most momentous developments in modern history." That growth was in part the result of the accelerating pace of scientific and technological progress—with some of the most important innovations of the Industrial Revolution (such as the automobile, the airplane, radios and telephones) just making their appearance—and that progress in turn generated a euphoria about the possibilities of scientific and human progress that was at least the equal of today's excitement about the Information Revolution.

The ends of both centuries have also been marked by great optimism about the prospects for peace as well. If anything, the experience of peace—or at least peace among the major powers—was longer and deeper at the end of the last century than it is in our time. There had been no wars between the major powers for nearly thirty years, there had been nothing comparable to the four decades of the Cold War, and it had been nearly a century—since the end of the Napoleonic Wars—that the world had experienced war on a global or continental scale.

Indeed, the worst experience of warfare in the last eighty-five years of the last century was the American Civil War. But at the turn of the century even that bloody tragedy was a fading memory. America's most recent experience of war at the century's end was the Spanish-American War, in which the United States acquired a Pacific empire through a war lasting less than three months. When Commodore George Dewey destroyed the Spanish fleet in Manila Bay in one morning, at the cost of only seven American seamen wounded, one newspaper headlined it as the "Greatest Naval Engagement of Modern Times."

The optimism of both periods is reflected also in writings about the future of warfare which expressed the hopeful expectation that economic and social changes were rendering war obsolete. In our time, that hope has been reflected in the popular reaction to such books as Francis Fukuyama's *The End of History* or John Mueller's *Retreat from Doomsday*.

At the end of the last century, Ivan Bloch—author of a six-volume work, *The Future of War,* which argued that war between the major powers had become impossible "except at the price of suicide" —persuaded the young Russian Czar Nicholas II to call for an arms limitation conference which convened in the Hague in 1899. Even more influential was Norman Angell's book *The Great Illusion,* which became a worldwide best-seller at the beginning of the twentieth century. The "illusion" of the title was the belief that nations could profit from war. Angell sought to demonstrate, to the contrary, that "war, even when victorious, can no longer achieve those aims for which peoples strive." The developments of the preceding forty years had "set up a financial interdependence of the capitals of the world, so complex [that it makes] New York dependent on London, London upon Paris, Paris upon Berlin, to a greater degree than has ever yet been the case in history." Should the German generals argue for war, the "influence of the whole finance of Germany would be brought to bear on the German Government to put an end to a situation ruinous to German trade."

As late as 1913, one of Angell's disciples, President David Starr Jordan of Stanford University argued that "the Great War of Europe, ever threatening,...will never come....The bankers will not find the money for such a fight, the industries will not maintain it, the statesmen cannot....There will be no general war." Angell received the Nobel Prize for Peace in 1933, the year the Nazis came to power.

THE RISE OF NEW POWERS AND
THE TRAGEDY OF THE TWENTIETH CENTURY

Of course, the twentieth century failed to realize the great promise with which it opened. Looking back on the turn of the century from the eve of a second world war, Winston Churchill wrote in 1938 that

> The scale on which events have shaped themselves [since 1895], has dwarfed the episodes of the Victorian Era....The smooth river with its eddies and ripples along which we then sailed, seems inconceivably remote from the cataract down which we have been hurled and the rapids in whose turbulence we are now struggling.

Something happened that caused the hopes for the new century to be dashed, something that we should consider as we try to manage the course of the world into the next century.

Alongside the remarkable and peaceful progress that was taking place at the end of the last century, the world was grappling with—or, more accurately, failing to manage—the emergence of major new powers. Not only was Japan newly powerful in Asia, but Germany, which had not even existed before the late 19th century, was becoming a dominant force in Europe. Today, the same spectacular economic growth which is reducing poverty, expanding trade and creating new middle classes is also creating new economic powers and possibly new military ones as well—a circumstance particularly true in Asia.

Smaller countries in Asia—such as Thailand, the Philippines, and Vietnam—are small only by Asian standards. With populations in the range of 60-80 million, these countries are comparable in size to the great powers of Europe; if they were to continue to grow at rates 4-6 percent faster than the big European countries, they would overtake them economically in the next two to four decades. Although such disparities in growth rates probably cannot be sustained as these countries approach European levels of productivity, the effects of their growing economic power will be felt long before they reach equality.

Those, of course, are among the smaller Asian countries. In China, three provinces are each larger than unified Germany. India is a country of 900 million people and a GDP of more than a trillion dollars, growing at better than 5 percent per year. Indonesia, with nearly 200 million people, is the fourth most populous country in the world. A unified Korea, which may be on the horizon, would be the size of a major European power; even without unification, South Korea alone is in the process of becoming one of the world's larger economies.

A number of other countries have the potential to be much stronger in twenty years, relative to the rest of the world, than they are now. Russia is the most obvious example. Although its present weakness might persist for some time, it certainly has the human resources to assume its place as one of the larger economies of Europe if it can finally create the conditions for stable investment in the Russian economy. Iran is likely to be a much more powerful country in ten-to-twenty years, if only because of its nuclear program. And several Latin American countries seem to have found the key to sustained economic growth, which could begin shifting the distribution of power within the Western Hemisphere in the next several decades.

Let us consider more carefully the situation of East Asia. The emergence of China by itself would present sizable problems; the emergence of China along with a number of other Asian powers presents an extremely complex equation. In the case of China, there is the additional problematic element of China's outsider status. The

obvious and disturbing analogy with the last turning of a century is
to the position of Germany, a country that felt it had been denied its
"place in the sun," a country that believed it had been mistreated by
the other powers and was determined to achieve its rightful place by
nationalistic assertiveness.

There are enormous differences, of course, between the Kaiser's
Germany and late-20th-century China. China is an old country,
recovering its strength, with a much longer history of involvement in
the world. Some would argue that the history of China's relatively
non-aggressive behavior when it was one of the world's dominant
powers (during the Sung and Ming dynasties) gives ground for
optimism that a newly powerful China will use its strength with
moderation.

But not all the differences are reassuring. China's real sense of
grievance at mistreatment by the European powers in the last century
and by Japan in this one has a much stronger foundation than
Germany's resentment. And in one other respect the similarities to
19th-century Germany should give us pause: China is going through
a transition from two decades of extremely skillful management of its
international relationships to a new leadership of uncertain quality. It
was just such a transition from the statesmanship of Bismarck to the
incompetence of his successors that was a principal factor leading to
the tragedy of the First World War.

And it is not only in China that a transition of this kind is on the
horizon. Over the next ten years, many of the leaders who have been
key in maintaining the extraordinary stability of Southeast Asia over
the last twenty years are likely to leave the scene. The new leaders
who will replace such men as Suharto, Lee Kuan Yew, Mahathir
Mohamed, Fidel Ramos or Thailand's King Bhumibol will have
difficulty improving on their overall record in maintaining regional
stability. If they fail to do as well, the effects on the rest of Asia,
particularly on China, could be very harmful.

The 20th century did not, of course, unfold as it appeared to
promise. By its midpoint it was already the bloodiest century in
history, and a very large fraction of that bloodshed can be attributed
ultimately to the failure to deal with the emergence of the new
powers—Germany in Europe, Japan in Asia. This failure led directly
to World War I, which was by itself an historic disaster of previously
unsurpassed proportions. World War I, in turn, planted the seeds of
Nazism in Germany and Bolshevism in Russia. The first led directly
to World War II and the Holocaust; the second led to the crimes of

Lenin and Stalin and of Pol Pot and to four decades of Cold War. In Asia, the failure to deal effectively with emerging Japanese power not only produced the expansion of World War II into the Pacific but was also responsible for half a century of horrors in China, some inflicted by the Japanese themselves and some by the Communist regime whose path to power was opened by the chaos caused by Japanese intervention.

The combined effect of all of these events was the violent death of tens of millions of people—more than we are able to count. The 20th century closes on a remarkably peaceful note, but it was the bloodiest century so far in human history. Many Europeans today would agree with the view that Boris Pasternak expresses through the voice of the character Lara in *Doctor Zhivago:*

> I believe now that the war is to blame for everything, for all the misfortunes that followed and that hound our generation to this day....I can still remember a time when we all accepted the peaceful outlook of the last century. It was taken for granted that you listened to reason....For a man to die by the hand of another was a rare, an exceptional event, something quite out of the ordinary. And then there was the jump from this peaceful, naive moderation to blood and tears, to mass insanity, and to the savagery of daily, hourly, legalized, rewarded slaughter....This social evil became an epidemic. It was catching. And it affected everything, nothing was left untouched by it.

Nothing decrees that history will repeat itself, not even in the sense of Marx's famous remark about the two Napoleons: "the first time as tragedy, the second time as farce." But if we are to realize the enormous promise of the coming century, we will have to do a better job of managing the emergence of new powers on the world scene. If we fail, the consequences could be even more destructive than we have seen in the twentieth century because the weapons of war have become even more terrible.

SOME CHARACTERISTICS OF THE EMERGING SYSTEM

One conclusion of this line of analysis is to note that it is still not possible to declare, pace Fukuyama, that history is at an end. But the reason for saying so is not simply because of the old ethnic rivalries that have emerged with the end of the Cold War, nor because of the phenomenon of "failed states." It is rather, and more seriously, because the possibility of war among major powers cannot be discounted, at least not before stable relationships with the new emerging powers have been developed.

It also seems dangerously premature to conclude that the "Age of Nonstate Actors" has arrived and that we are witnessing what Jessica Tuchman Mathews calls a "continuing diffusion of power away from nation-states." This is not to deny that advances in communications and information technology, and the increasing mobility of capital as well as goods, are increasing the importance of a wide range of non-state actors, from NGOs to multinational corporations to international criminal networks. But the developments under discussion here are also increasing the importance of new state actors, and it is not clear which of these trends is dominant. There are potential interactions between the two, as for example in the possible use of international terrorist and criminal networks by states. Moreover, some of the strengthening of transnational institutions in the wake of the Cold War is a product of the decline of competition among states. That trend could be reversed—for example, we could see a weakening of international organizations—if competition among major powers were to become intense again.

Most fundamentally, it is, for the most part, the relations among state actors that will determine the question of war or peace (although civil wars will remain significant). While the power of states may diminish in many other areas, this issue is still paramount. Moreover, the new technologies which make it possible for non-state actors to organize and communicate in new ways may also have a revolutionary impact on military technology at the state level (more on this later).

A third conclusion, in reflecting on the experience of the past century, is that the greatest danger may lie less in a new Cold War than in an opposition of coalitions. In fact, both World War I and World War II resulted from the emergence of revisionist coalitions. Alone, any of the newly emerging powers (including China) may be a long way from being able to challenge the United States, much less a coalition of the democracies. But a group of new powers might be able to present such a challenge much sooner. One can conceive of a world in which revisionist ambitions in China, Russia and Iran might lead those countries to ally themselves in opposition to the international status quo, even though their individual aims might differ greatly or even, in part, conflict. One objective of Trilateral diplomacy must be to prevent that kind of hostile coalition from forming.

A fourth characteristic of the emerging system is that power is gradually shifting: from Europe and North America to Asia and, to a lesser extent, to Latin America; and within Asia from Japan to the developing countries of the region and particularly to China. Power, in short, is shifting away from the Trilateral countries. The process is still, of course, at a relatively early stage. It will be several decades before the developing countries of Asia really catch up with the advanced economies, even if they can continue to sustain their much higher growth rates. It will take even longer if they experience periods of difficulty, as Thailand is now for example, and growth rates are likely to slow as per capita productivity approaches the level of the advanced countries.

However, even with these qualifications, the change under way is an enormous one. Although it is gradual, it is happening much faster than similar developments of the previous two centuries. The changes will begin to be felt long before the new distribution of power is complete. And while there may be some slowing in the relative growth rates, there is no reason any longer to think there are cultural or natural limitations that might keep these countries from eventually reaching the per-capita-productivity levels of the advanced countries, and thus attaining an economic weight that corresponds to their enormous populations.

A fifth feature of this emerging system is a mirror image of the previous two: for some time to come, the advanced democracies of Europe, North America and Japan will have the great preponderance of economic power. If they can coordinate their policies with some effectiveness they may provide a powerful base on which to integrate the newly emerging countries, including China, into a stable international system. But that preponderance is almost certainly a wasting asset. Twenty or thirty years may seem like a long time, but it is a relatively short period of history for changes of this magnitude to take place. If we don't make good use of the next ten years, events may begin to spin out of our control.

Sixth, it is important to note that the economic changes transforming new countries into major powers are also likely to change them internally. In this respect, I think that Frank Fukuyama is substantially right (even though the conclusion may be dangerous if applied prematurely). Although Asian democracy may be different from European or American, the evidence is powerful that as nations become richer it becomes increasingly difficult to govern them by non-democratic means. The developments that are strengthening non-state actors reinforce this conclusion.

If the new powers do become more democratic, they are likely also to have a larger stake in preserving the status quo. The evidence to support this conclusion is more ambiguous. Although it is difficult to find examples of democracies fighting wars against one another, it is not difficult to find examples of democracies, including the United States, behaving with bellicose aggressiveness. A China that is governed more democratically might, for example, have a foreign policy that would reflect popular nationalist pressures. Perhaps it is significant that in the recent controversy over the Senkaku (or Diaoyu) Islands, the Beijing regime took a more restrained position than democratic elements in Hong Kong. On balance, however, I believe a China that governs its own people by force is more likely to try to govern its neighbors by force; and a China that is governed democratically is more likely to reflect popular desires to enjoy the prosperity that is only possible with peace.

Henry Rowen has suggested that China will probably be more or less democratic by the year 2015. Supposing that is true, and supposing that a new distribution of power will be much easier to manage with a democratic China, that makes the next twenty years a very crucial period. Twenty years is a short time from the perspective of history, but it represents the normal lifetime of two leadership generations in most of the democracies.

IMPLICATIONS FOR TRILATERAL COOPERATION

There are a number of implications for Trilateral cooperation that flow from the above analysis.

First is the need for the United States to continue to play a balancing role in Europe and, particularly, in Asia. In fact, this is not a new role. Even during the Cold War, the American security role was important not only in containing the Soviet Union but in maintaining regional balance as well, particularly in East Asia. Without the American role, it is questionable whether Japan and South Korea could have overcome their historic antagonisms sufficiently to function as de facto security partners. Nor would the other countries of East Asia have reacted with relative calm to Japan's still quite modest efforts to maintain a self-defense capability. Perhaps the most striking illustration of the American role in a complex Asian security equation was in the response to Vietnam's invasion of Cambodia, when the United States provided support to an improbable coalition of China and the non-Communist countries of Southeast Asia in their efforts to contain the Soviet Union's Vietnamese ally. This ability to assemble ad hoc coalitions against efforts to disturb the status quo may be increasingly important as the Asian security equation becomes more complex over the next two decades.

However, this type of role requires a flexibility that may be harder for the United States to maintain than a position of sustained opposition to a clearly identified threat. Moreover, it is a much more difficult role to explain and defend to the American public. During the Cold War, opposition to Soviet expansion provided a widely accepted rationale for a much broader US security role. The problem of domestic support will become much more serious when, as seems likely, Korea is eventually unified. While a continuing alliance with the United States would make a great deal of strategic sense for a country finding itself between China and Japan, and while American interests would certainly be well-served by maintaining stability in Northeast Asia, the American public is likely to ask what the threat is, precisely, that we are defending against. It is hard to imagine arguing that, for example, a US commitment might help to prevent military competition or conflict between our Korean and Japanese allies, conflict which might draw in China. But fuzzier rationales, like the need to maintain stability, are less convincing. Challenged to explain the threat that NATO faced right after the Berlin Wall came down, President Bush answered that "the threat is uncertainty...the threat is instability"—to which his critics responded by asking "how many divisions does instability have?"

A second important conclusion is that, since the Western countries taken as a group will still retain the preponderance of economic power for a considerable time, cooperation among them will be important in managing the transition to a new distribution of power. Although the purpose of such cooperation is strategic, the cooperation required is not primarily military. In fact, the ability to apply the combined economic leverage of the Trilateral countries on important issues may be one of the best ways to avoid military confrontations.

Take, for example, the issue of Hong Kong, one of the most important near-term challenges to the development of a new equilibrium in Asia. At its most positive, a successful reintegration of Hong Kong into China would be reassuring to China's neighbors, especially Taiwan, and might even begin to nudge China's evolution in a more positive direction. On the other hand, if China were to renege on its promise of "one country, two systems" and to pressure Hong Kong to go backwards toward a system that is more like the rest of China, there would be many negative effects, including on China's relations with the United States and perhaps with other Trilateral nations.

The greatest threat to the West-West cooperation that is so essential may come from the intense competition for economic advantage among the Trilateral countries. If China finds that it can pick off the Western countries one by one, awarding contracts to Airbus when it doesn't like American policy or using Japan to block pressure from international financial institutions or playing Western countries off to dictate the terms of WTO admission, none of us will have much influence. And the failure to find effective ways of influencing China will lead to more public pressure in the United States—and perhaps in some other Trilateral countries as well—to confront China in ways that are likely to be both ineffective and provocative.

Avoiding such a course requires a recognition by all the advanced democracies that something more than commercial advantage is at stake. It requires a recognition by Europeans that developments in Asia, remote as they may appear, are matters not merely of regional concern but of global strategic concern as well. It requires Japan to take a leadership profile on issues of political concern, and not to use legitimate concern about exciting historical animosities as an excuse for pursuing exclusively commercial policies. And it requires a willingness by the United States to accept the compromises that are necessary to produce a common political agenda, rather than indulging in political posturing that may be more emotionally satisfying but less effective.

A third conclusion is that the values which the Trilateral countries share can become an important instrument in shaping the transition to a new distribution of power. A commitment to larger political purposes should be part of the glue that binds the advanced democracies together and allows them to shape a future that can assure their continued safety and prosperity. Unlike Professor Huntington, I do not believe those values are exclusively "Western," in his narrower sense. At their summit meeting in Malta eight years ago, Mikhail Gorbachev pleaded with President Bush to stop talking about Western values and to say democratic values instead. It was a request Bush readily agreed to. In fact, it is the appeal of those values to great numbers of people in countries that are not yet democratic that is one of our most powerful tools for shaping the emerging world.

This doesn't mean that we can dictate the course of political development in other countries. Our ability to influence may often be quite modest. If we are not careful, our influence may even be negative, as would be the case if the United States were to revoke MFN for China. Such a move would not only damage American economic interests, it would also damage Taiwan, Hong Kong and the growing private sector within China itself, which are among the most important forces that have the potential to move China in a more democratic direction.

However, while the Clinton Administration may have played its hand badly with China in the first few years in the way it attempted to pursue human rights objectives, it would be a serious mistake now to drop human rights considerations entirely, as the Administration sometimes seems in danger of doing. The first key to a successful pursuit of the strategic objective of a more democratic China is the recognition that this will take time to come about and that it will primarily be a product of forces within China itself. Within that framework, however, we can help to push change in the right direction—if we can develop leverage that is more carefully targeted, if we can coordinate policies better among the Western countries, and if we do not present our objectives as fundamental challenges to the regime.

A fourth conclusion I would draw is that there is still a need for the basic alliance structure that was created for other purposes during the Cold War. This is particularly true in Asia, even though it is most often in reference to Asia that one hears the argument that those alliance relationships need to be replaced by some new multilateral structure of collective security. One line of argument says that in the post-Cold War era we should do away with security relationships that divide countries of the region. Another says that the United States simply can't afford to continue shouldering this leadership role.

In fact, new multilateral security arrangements have little chance of working unless they are built on the foundations of the strong alliance relationships constructed in an earlier period. To those who say the United States can't afford it anymore, I would say that the United States can't afford not to. In fact, because of the greatly reduced threats in both Europe and Asia, the United States is able to sustain credible military commitments at greatly reduced costs, including overall personnel reductions of more than 500,000 and real expenditure reductions of nearly 50 percent, with the US defense burden down to about 3 percent of GNP, less than half of the Cold War level.

There are important ways, however, in which these Cold War structures can be complemented by new ones that bring together countries that did not have the experience of cooperating with one another or which may even have been adversaries. One of these is the

ASEAN Regional Forum (ARF), which brings the ASEAN countries together with all of the major powers in the Asia Pacific region in a forum where it is possible to discuss common problems.

However, while ARF is a useful forum for discussion, it may be too large for actually resolving issues. For that purpose, one potentially useful mechanism would be the greater use of trilateral mechanisms which would allow parties to discuss problems of serious common concern in an environment in which their bilateral disputes are muted. For example, the United States, Japan and Russia could work together on common concerns about security in the Northwest Pacific; or China, Japan, and the United States might develop an agenda of common security problems to work on. While the United States would fit logically into a great many such groupings, there is no reason why it would have to be in all of them. In fact, an overlapping network of such arrangements might help to prevent any clear fault line from dividing one group of countries from another.

THE CHALLENGE OF PRESERVING THE PEACE

Preserving the peace is not the only challenge the Trilateral countries must meet to realize the great promise of the next century. But preventing war among the major powers, particularly nuclear powers, is critical to success in everything that we hope to achieve.

If we can sustain Trilateral cooperation, we will have a strong base from which to tackle the specific challenges we face. These include: (1) getting Asia right; (2) getting Russia right; (3) mastering the revolution in military technology; (4) preserving energy security (or getting the Persian Gulf and Central Asia right); (5) getting the right relationship with the Moslem world; and (6) reducing the role of nuclear weapons. Each of these could be an essay by itself. Let me confine myself to a few observations on the first three.

Getting Asia Right

Getting Asia right means getting China right, but it means much more than that. In fact, there is a danger of becoming so mesmerized by China's importance that we neglect the rest of Asia. It was reported in *Business Week* several months ago that Sandy Berger—since promoted to be President Clinton's National Security Advisor—had privately expressed the view that China is now the most important country in Asia for the United States, a report that naturally caused concern in Japan. If true, however, Mr. Berger would not be the first senior

American official to get this wrong. It has been a recurring problem ever since the US opening to China twenty-five years ago left the Japanese reeling from the Nixon *shokku.*

Important though China is, an overemphasis on China is a mistake for several reasons:

- First, the rest of Asia is enormously important by itself. Americans frequently seem to forget that Japan and the other countries of East Asia have a combined population of nearly 700 million people and a combined GNP (measured in PPP terms) of more than $5 trillion. And that does *not* include the 900 million people of India or any of the other countries of *South* Asia. (In fact, we need to start paying more attention to India.)

- Second, many of the other countries of East Asia are much more natural partners of the United States and other Trilateral countries. This is true particularly for those countries that share democratic values with us, but it is also true for those who share our interest in the maintenance of a peaceful status quo in the region and in the non-violent settlement of disputes.

- Finally, US relations with China have generally been better when US relations with the rest of Asia, particularly with Japan, have been good. It is not a matter of slighting China or underestimating China's importance but rather of keeping some balance in our dealings with China.

In fact, there is a need for balance in a larger sense in US dealings with China. *Both* sides have to work at making the relationship work. Having made the mistake of behaving as though it could dictate to China, the Clinton Administration should not now go overboard in the opposite direction. As important as China is to the Trilateral countries, the Trilateral countries are just as important to China. When we forget this, we are not likely to bargain effectively with the Chinese; and the relationship with China is very much a matter of bargaining and negotiating, a point that the rather bland term "engaging" tends to obscure.

Our dealings with China should incorporate three different elements: (1) As much emphasis as possible on *cooperation,* including on specific issues where we share common interests (such as avoiding war in Korea or promoting the independence of the Central Asian republics) and a more general willingness to treat China as the important country that it is and to welcome it as a partner in developing the international system; (2) tough *bargaining* on issues where we disagree, which requires an ability to marshall leverage, so that we can relate our responsiveness to Chinese concerns to their responsiveness to ours; and (3) *opposition to the use of force,* which does not have to be explicit most of the time but which should always be very clear.

This third point applies to the case of Taiwan, where there is still no better policy than continuation of the two principles on which the US approach has rested for more than two decades: opposition to the use of force and opposition to attempts by either side to impose an outcome unilaterally, including specific opposition to a unilateral assertion of independence by Taiwan. The purpose of this is to buy time during which the differences between the two can be settled peacefully. While we should encourage any steps they make in that direction, the paradox is that the less we get directly involved between them the more likely they are to make progress.

Perhaps the *most* difficult issue in China's relations with the Trilateral countries for some time to come will be the issue of human rights. It is made more difficult by the fact that China is going through a dual political crisis: a *crisis of succession* over what leadership will replace Deng Xiaoping and a *crisis of legitimacy* caused by absence of belief in the Marxist doctrine on which the Communist Party still bases its claim to rule 1.2 billion Chinese people. It is this second crisis that is the most serious in the long run. We do not want to act in ways that might make it easier for the leadership to reach for militant nationalism as an alternative basis for legitimacy. But we do have an interest in promoting an evolution of China toward a more pluralist and less personalized political system.

Is there anything that we can do to encourage this movement? Again, paradoxically, we can do more if we recognize that our influence is limited. We should posture ourselves to be allies of those who want to promote change, not appear to be opponents of the entire regime or of a strong China in any form. We need to continue to criticize, but not every criticism should be accompanied by specific threats of punishment. In fact, if we want to make progress, the Chinese leadership must be able to claim that it is acting voluntarily. However, the Chinese know well that "one hand washes the other." While specific linkage should be avoided, there *should* be a broad relationship between China's political evolution and the warmth of the overall relationship. Most critical in this respect over the next few years will be China's treatment of Hong Kong.

Getting Russia Right

Getting Russia right depends on the Russians themselves getting the right view of Russia's role in the world. The most positive outcome—and one that we should try hard to promote—is a Russia that sees its interests advanced by concentrating on development and security within its new borders. A Russia that thinks its future lies in reestablishing the Czarist or Soviet empire in Europe would clash with the West, even if NATO did not take in new members. A Russia that gets bogged down intervening in Central Asia will relearn what the French learned in Algeria and what the Russians should have learned from Afghanistan and Chechnya.

But a Russia that tries to develop as a great nation within its new borders will face real security problems, not from NATO but from other directions. We are told that the Russians can't accept NATO expansion because they have an image of NATO that was created by four decades of propaganda by the old Soviet regime. It is time, to paraphrase the late Senator Fulbright, to replace that old myth with the new reality of a Russia that has enormous common interests with the Trilateral countries in promoting stability in Asia, particularly in East Asia.

We should welcome Russia as a significant Pacific power into APEC. We should involve Russia in resolution of issues of Northeast Asian security, such as Korea. We should work to develop as much cooperation as possible between Russia and Japan and try to find ways to do this even before the issue of Japan's Northern Territories is resolved. And, just as we leaned toward China when it appeared that it was threatened by the former Soviet Union, we should be prepared to lean toward Russia if it is threatened along its long border with China.

Mastering the Revolution in Military Technology

The technological changes that are transforming the world's economy also have the potential to transform military affairs. The world saw a glimpse of this during the Persian Gulf War. But the technologies that were demonstrated there with such dramatic effect are in fact technologies of the 1970s. The pace of change since then, as we know from civilian applications, is truly extraordinary and shows every sign of continuing. This could revolutionize warfare as much as the changes of the 1920s and 1930s did in an earlier period.

That earlier history suggests three important conclusions for our time:

- First, as the German experience demonstrates, a country that masters this kind of technological revolution, when others fail to, can possess military strength far out of proportion to its economic power.
- Second, the advantage in a competition of this kind does not simply go to those who invent the new technologies—the British and French, after all, were the first to invent tanks and fielded almost as many as the Germans at the time of the Battle of France. The advantage goes to those who figure out how to apply new technology in new and decisive ways. And the advantage in this kind of competition, as in much commercial competition, often goes to the innovative and hungry upstarts rather than the stodgy and complacent leaders.
- Third, unlike armored warfare, whose development was confined to military establishments (although related technologies, such as radios and combustion engines had a parallel civilian development), many of today's technologies with military application are also being developed rapidly in the commercial sector. Thus, the possibility of commercial advances being purchased or otherwise acquired for military use is a more serious one.

These considerations have two implications for the Trilateral countries. First is the need to sustain innovation in military technology and in the operational employment of new technologies. Although the United States and its allies have a commanding lead at present, investment in new systems will come under increasing pressure from the many demands (such as for peacekeeping) on declining budgets. Moreover, complacency about our "lead" could stifle innovation. Second, it may be necessary to consider controls over some of the most advanced commercial technologies, despite the enormous political and technical difficulties in making such controls effective.

THE NEED FOR PUBLIC SUPPORT

This essay has presented a formidable set of challenges, and it is fair to ask whether the Trilateral countries are capable of meeting them, particularly when the public seems relatively uninterested in questions of foreign policy. Even though the immediate impact of individual foreign policy decisions may be small, the stakes involved in successful long-term management of the changes taking place in the world are enormous. It is no exaggeration to say that the safety of our children and grandchildren depends on it. It is important for leaders in the democracies to argue effectively for sound policies and not to assume, mistakenly, that the public simply can't understand foreign policy concerns.

As a counterexample, a large fraction of the American public has been persuaded that something must be done about the budget deficit "for the sake of our children and grandchildren." While that concern may not always prevail when it conflicts with more immediate interests, the degree to which it has shaped the domestic debate is remarkable. Why can't an equally effective argument be made for the need to pay attention to foreign policy, so that the next century—the century of our children and grandchildren—does not become the bloodiest century in history? If the stakes were more widely understood, the terms of debate on a host of specific issues might be different.

Public support is particularly important in sustaining the North Atlantic Alliance and the US-Japan and US-Korea alliances, and in continuing the American security commitments to Europe and Asia on which those alliances depend. This conclusion seems to come as a disappointment to those who thought the end of the Cold War would mean that these alliances were no longer needed; to those who thought we could not afford the expense; to those who thought we should return to a more "natural" state of things in which the Europeans managed their own affairs (and perhaps Asians did likewise?); or to those who hoped for something more novel to replace the institutional arrangements of the Cold War.

For those of us, on the other hand, who recognize that these alliances are still essential, it comes as a pleasant surprise that the American commitment is as strong as it appears to be more than seven years after the fall of the Berlin Wall. There seems to be no debate about maintaining US troops in Europe at their new, appropriately reduced, level. Indeed, NATO is performing a new mission in the Balkans with some measure of success, and there is bipartisan support in both the US Congress and the Executive Branch for the alliance to bring in new members. In Asia, the Clinton Administration has promised to maintain US troops at their current level of roughly 100,000, and the strategic importance of the US-Japan alliance was reaffirmed during President Clinton's visit to Japan in April 1996. China's belligerent conduct in the Taiwan Strait earlier that year increased public support for the US-Japan alliance in both countries, particularly in Japan.

Yet these indications of continued American support for the alliances may not be as solid as they appear. These American commitments would be coming under much stronger challenge if the partisan politics were reversed, as was the case in the 1980s, with a Republican President and a Democratic Congress. Moreover, even though the Congressional Republicans have been strongly supportive of US commitments to its allies, that support will probably weaken as the older members, those with a deeper commitment to America's leadership role, leave the scene.

Challenges to these commitments could come from a number of directions. Already the US Secretary of Defense is placing an arbitrary time limit on the US commitment in Bosnia, saying that if the parties there want to "go back to slaughtering each other," that is "up to them." Elsewhere, pressures on the US defense budget will make it increasingly difficult to maintain present troop levels in both Europe and Asia. While it may have been a mistake to measure the level of US commitment in terms of the number of personnel deployed —particularly when new technology has the potential to make smaller forces more effective—it will be difficult to avoid the appearance that reductions, even militarily insignificant ones, represent a weakening of American commitment. Finally there is the danger, particularly with Japan, that trade disputes will once again lead people to denigrate the importance of the strategic relationship, as happened in the first years of the Clinton Administration.

Maintaining public support in the face of these challenges will not be easy. It will require demonstrations that the members of the alliances are capable of putting longer-term common interests ahead of short-term special interests, demonstrations that will be harder as long as people believe that the threat to the common interests is rather remote or even non-existent. America's allies seem to believe that the United States is behaving like a hegemonial bully, now that it is the sole remaining superpower. The American people, on the other hand, believe that our allies are taking a "free ride" at our expense and that America's relative share of the burden has actually increased since the end of the Cold War when it should have declined. These gaps in perception may be difficult to bridge, but the consequences of a failure to do so could be serious indeed.